WALKS IN THE KENDAL AREA

(Series 3) - 2nd Edition

FOREWORD

This new edition of **Walks in the Kendal Area** - Series 3 has been comprehensively updated. Two of the old walks have been replaced by new ones in little used areas, giving further opportunities to link two walks together. The emphasis is again on clear descriptions of how to find your way, so please read the text carefully. We hope that the maps and text have been made easier to follow by the introduction of paragraph numbers. If you want to follow the route on an OS map (though this shouldn't be necessary) we recommend the purchase of the recently introduced two sided edition of the 1:25,000 Outdoor Leisure Map No.7 (Southeast Lakeland) which is priced at £5.95. This covers all but walks Nos. 15, 16 and parts of 13 and 18. All walks are circular except No 18.

Sandwiched as we are in the Kendal area between the Lake District and Yorkshire Dales National Parks our high quality landscape is under increasing pressure from developments that would not be permitted in the parks. Whatever you think about the desirability of windfarms and telecommunication masts, these are developments that perhaps have most impact on ramblers. Should current windfarm proposals be agreed, many of the walks in this series of books will be affected. We hope this won't spoil your enjoyment. The good news is that if it's solitude that you are looking for, you can still do nearly all of these walks without meeting another person. All walks are on rights of way unless otherwise stated.

Published by The Kendal Group of the Ramblers Association
1999

The name and address of current Secretary
can be obtained from Kendal Library
or from the Ramblers Yearbook under 'Lake District'.

Key map for the location of walks

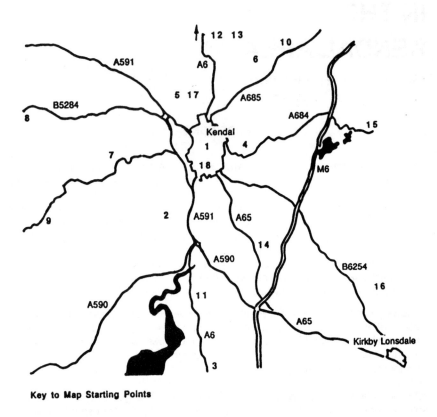

Key to Map Starting Points

Cover photograph:	Kendal Castle
	Tim Baynes
Maps*:	David Walsh
Sketches and photographs	Group members

* Maps based on OS 1:25,000 series with permission of HM Stationery Office.

CONTENTS

Clapper Bridge, Crosthwaite   Ian Brodie

3

WALK NO. 1
The Town of Kendal
6.5km (4 miles)

This route, using mainly footpaths within the central area of the town, will give walkers a general idea of the topography of Kendal and some excellent views of the surrounding countryside. For those wishing to learn more about the history and architecture of the town there are many publications available at the Town Hall information office. An up to date street plan, which could be useful, is also available from there.

Start at the wrought iron gates in front of the Parish Church, at the south end of the main street (car park near by). Cross the road and go up Kirkbarrow Lane, a narrow ginnel known locally as t'Crack, next to the Wheatsheaf Inn, with views northwards, in winter, to Castle Howe, which you will visit shortly. At the end, turn right and cross over into Buttery Well Road, continuing with the children's playground on your left. Go straight over the next crossroads to reach Gillingate through a pedestrian access. The route continues as Buttery Well Lane across the road, going alongside some old peoples' bungalows to reach Captain French Lane. Turn left and

UP T'CRACK   M.Adams

almost immediately right into a steep walled path or ginnel, known as Garth Heads. After about 50m go up the steep steps on the left. (A little further along on the right is the garden door leading down to the Brewery Arts Centre, where refreshments can be obtained.) The steep steps lead up to a track across the near edge of the open green of Bowling Fell, site of the motte and bailey Castle Howe, the earlier and less well known of Kendal's two castles. The motte is surmounted by an obelisk erected in 1788 to commemorate the centenary of the 1688 Revolution leading to the abdication of James II.

1   Having explored Bowling Fell return to the track along its edge and follow it northwards between houses to Beast Banks, a very old part of Kendal where animals were once baited before slaughter and butchery. Turn right down the steep hill, and cross the road to follow the pavement round left into Low Fellside, which marks the eastern boundary of Fellside, once a notorious slum area, but now redeveloped and modernised, retaining many of the old ginnels and steps. Walk up the cobbled Sepulchre Lane on your immediate left, passing an old Quaker cemetery on the left at the bend; pass Cliff Brow and Church Terrace and go up the next steps on the left to reach the junction of Serpentine Road and Queens Road. Cross over Queens Road and enter Serpentine Woods by the path to the left of Serpentine Cottage. Keep bearing right at the path junctions, to go alongside a small tree nursery, gradually climbing through the woods, eventually to emerge

through a wide gap in the end wall onto the open fellside. From here there is a wide view of the upper Kent valley, the eastern Lakeland fells and the skyline round to the Howgill fells, with Kendal and Benson Knott in the foreground.

2   From this flat open space aim slightly right and downhill towards a clump of mature beech and pine trees, then drop steeply down to a track running alongside a wall, and a stile in the wall just below the trees, leading into the corner of a field. Through the stile you can take a short cut by going half left downhill, aiming for the trees in the corner, to join another right of way going alongside the wall above the allotments.   Pass through the small gates on top of the stile near the trees and turn right, past the remains of an old barn, and through a gateway to join a path down beside the wall on the right.   Before reaching the locked iron gate at the bottom of this path go through a stile and small gate in the wall and follow the track down to Windermere Road.

3   Turn left, then cross the busy road with great care into Fairfield Lane opposite. This gives access to Kendal Green, an open space of considerable interest. Cross the green on the metalled track and go straight ahead to a drive between houses that leads to Horncop Lane. Turn left for about 150m to a footpath sign on the right, where a small gate gives access to a path down to Ashleigh Road. Follow the road right, to its junction with Burneside Road opposite Webb's Garden Centre, where refreshments may be obtained.

4   Go left along Burneside Road (or right if leaving the garden centre), then turn first right, down Dockray Hall Road. By bearing slightly right you gain access to Dockray Hall Walk beside the River Kent. Follow the river downstream to Victoria Bridge, crossing the road here and continuing on the same bank to Stramongate Bridge. Now go left, over the bridge and straight along Wildman Street, noting on the left the Castle Dairy, Kendal's oldest house. This dates from at least the 14th Century and is now a restaurant. At the road junction and pedestrian crossing further on, turn right into Ann Street. At the far end turn left into Castle Street, and then second right into Castle Road - Kendal's oldest municipal cemetery is on the corner. About 100m up Castle Road is a footpath sign to Kendal Castle on the right. Go through the kissing gate and go straight ahead up the shoulder of the hill to the castle, the later and better known of Kendal's two castles. Quite apart from its historical interest, particularly its associations with Katherine Parr, the last and surviving wife of Henry VIII, the drumlinoid hill on which it stands provides fine views of Kendal, with Scout Scar on the western horizon.

5   After exploring the castle ruins follow the path round the embankment on the town side to descend by a grassy path and cobbled steps to a kissing gate leading to Sunnyside, with Fletcher Park on the left. Continue down the road, crossing on the way the bridge that carries the road over the former Lancaster canal (now a cycle route), which was here nearing its northern end. On reaching the main road cross slightly right to Jennings Yard Footbridge over the Kent. After crossing this it is a pleasant walk through the riverside gardens of Abbott Hall to the Art Gallery, the museum of Lakeland Life and Industry, the Parish Church and the starting point of the walk

A Walk from Helsington Church   7.2km (4.5miles)

St John's Church, Helsington is the Parish Church of Brigsteer and is remarkable for its isolated position on the edge of the limestone escarpment overlooking the Lyth Valley. The views to the Lakeland Fells and Morecambe Bay are magnificent. The Wheatsheaf Inn at Brigsteer, the village visited on the walk, is a good stopping place if refreshments are required. The grid reference for the church is SD489889, and it is reached from the Kendal to Brigsteer road by turning off left soon after the road starts to descend the scarp. There is room for parking in front of the church except during Sunday services.

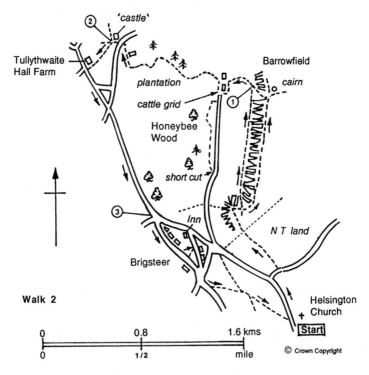

Start
Walk back along the track to the road, and then go uphill for a short distance to the footpath sign on the left pointing to Scout Scar. Follow the broad grassy track to the gate at the end of the National Trust land, and continue through the gate until the track turns sharp right and descends into a small valley. Follow the narrow path left, down the valley, continuing along the foot of the scar through woodland, with a wall on the left, until reaching a gate. (An alternative route, which may appeal more on a clear day or if the bracken is high, crosses the small valley and takes the track

which continues along the top of the scar. At a large cairn, opposite the farm below, a clear path descends the scar to the gate mentioned above.)

1   Cross the field towards Barrowfield Farm on the cart track beside the wall on your right, and follow the waymarked route around the outside of the farm buildings. On reaching the farm drive turn right then follow the sign pointing left in front of the farmhouse, going downhill and into the wood by a stile. (You could take a short cut on reaching the farm drive - see map). After going through the wood, cross a field to another stile and enter a plantation. Follow the path straight ahead through the plantation, ignoring all cross-paths, until you reach a forestry road. Turn right then left after 30m to follow roughly the line of the overhead power lines until the path descends via a left and right turn to reach a gate into a field. Cross the field to the left of the house, skirting around the old orchard to reach a track going right, to join the house drive. On reaching the road turn left for about 70m and go through the first field gate on the right, entering a field near a small barn, locally known as 'the Castle', a clue to its probable history.

2   Follow the track by the wall and go through a gateway on the left into the next field (ignoring the wall stile ahead), and on towards the farm buildings at Tullythwaite Hall. Keep round the left of the buildings to emerge onto the road by a stile near the end of the farm drive. Turn left along the road for 1.75km.

3   When you reach a four way junction at the edge of Brigsteer village go straight ahead onto the minor road and follow this for about 170m to a narrow path on the left that starts opposite the first house on the right. The walled path leads steeply up left to another road. Along this road to the left is the Wheatsheaf Inn, which serves bar meals, etc. but the walk continues to the right. Follow the road through the village, ignoring all side roads, until near the end of the village you reach a footpath sign on the left, to the church. Follow the path up to a gated stile, then bear diagonally right uphill to reach another stile in the top right-hand corner of the field, leading onto an unmetalled track. Turn right along the track and after about 120m look for a steep and narrow path slanting up through the wood on the left. This leads via a stile to the open fell below Helsington Church, which you'll soon see among the trees on the skyline.

BARROWFIELD FARM.

P. Standish

Beetham, Slackhead and the Fairy Steps   7.2km (4.5miles)

This is mainly a woodland walk, exploring part of the Arnside and Silverdale Area of Outstanding Natural Beauty. Starting from the historic village of Beetham with its ancient church and working watermill, the route passes the medieval pele tower of Beetham Hall, crosses some rare limestone pavements and visits the famous 'Fairy Steps'. Park in the southernmost of the two roads into Beetham from the A6 (SD497795). The smooth limestone paths can be very slippery.

Start
Follow the signpost pointing to Hale up the path beside the telephone kiosk. The path goes along the back of the houses to a kissing gate leading into a field. Head diagonally across the field half left, to reach a stone squeeze stile in the corner above Beetham Hall Farm and its medieval pele tower. Go along the bottom of the wood to another stile. Continue just outside the wood but above the outcrops, to reach a short green lane leading out of the corner of the field. On reaching a wall corner follow the sign to Slackhead along the Limestone Link Path, (a 15mile route between Arnside and Kirkby Lonsdale). Go straight ahead at the cross paths after a few metres. The path goes uphill through the woods. Look out for yellow waymarks over the next 800metres. Along this stretch the path goes through an area of fine limestone pavement, a rare and protected habitat for a variety of plants growing in the 'grykes' between the 'clints'. Care is needed in crossing this.

1   On reaching the road turn right and follow it for 500m, past a junction on the left, to a signpost on the left pointing to Storth and the Fairy Steps. Still on the Limestone Link path, follow the path between the cottages and onto a broad track through open woodland to reach a cross path and a four-pointed sign on a little cairn (this point will be visited again towards the end of the walk - take note!) Take the path to the left, to the Fairy Steps and Hazelslack.

2   The track goes up through a plantation of tall conifers and emerges onto a limestone scarp with fine views towards the Kent estuary and Arnside Knott, especially when the trees are bare. Straight ahead are the 'Fairy Steps', a narrow cleft in the rocks of the scarp, through which you have to squeeze to continue on the path. (An alternative route is available, by going some 400m along the scarp to the right and descending to a lower path that joins the main one below the steps).

3   Follow the sign to Hazelslack, down through the woods to a second and lesser scarp through which there is another, wider cleft, with man-made steps at right angles to the path. This is part of the 'coffin' route to Beetham, for burial in the days before there was a church at Arnside. Continue on down through Underlaid wood to reach a gate. Cross two fields, with a wall on the left, to the road near Hazelslack lower Farm and it's 14th Century pele tower.

4   On reaching the road, leave the Limestone Link path and turn right for 250m to a stile and footpath sign on the right. Over the stile bear slightly left, off the cart track, to another stone stile in a corner of the field, and then continue by the wall

on the left along two fields. Cross the far corner of the second field to a stile beside a gate and go through a narrow neck of woodland to another field.

5　Bear half right to a wooden stile leading into the woods again. Through the stile ignore the wide track straight ahead and follow the narrow path half left through the trees, the right of way. This leads to a clearing with signs of forestry use. Bear left through the clearing on a rough vehicular track that leads shortly to a more important forestry road. Turn right at the junction and after about 100m, where the road curves right, leave it for a narrower path going straight ahead. Climb up through the wood, going through a narrow gate in an old deer fence, eventually reaching some open grassland on Beetham Fell. Here you will find another small cairn with direction indicators on top.

6　Take the path towards Beetham, on a more pronounced track. As you re-enter the wood, just before the path goes through a broken wall, turn left down an indistinct path through the trees, and shortly go over a stile in the wall on the right. Continue following the path steeply downhill, passing between a field for pheasant rearing on the left and a large beech tree on the right, until the cairn mentioned earlier in the walk is reached. At this point turn left, signed Beetham, and almost immediately fork right, leaving a track to the left marked Private. About 100m after going through a gap in another ruined wall, and just before a left-hand bend, turn sharp left on a narrower path. This soon goes left again, round the wall of a derelict cottage garden, and comes to a stile in front of the cottage. Cross the stile and continue down through the wood and along its boundary to find another stile leading to the fields above Beetham village. Go down the field to the road and turn right to reach the Wheatsheaf Inn, the church and the start of the walk.

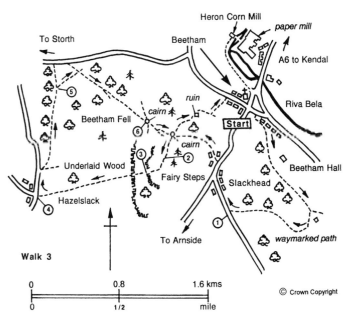

Walk 3

0　　　　0.8　　　　1.6 kms
0　　　　1/2　　　　mile

© Crown Copyright

9

WALK NO.4

Spindle Wood and Paddy Lane   8km (5 miles)

Spindle Wood is now only a remnant of what it must once have been, but its beautiful mature trees do much to enhance the views across the town from the east. Paddy Lane marks the eastern boundary of Kendal for a good part of its length and gives fine views towards the Lakeland fells.

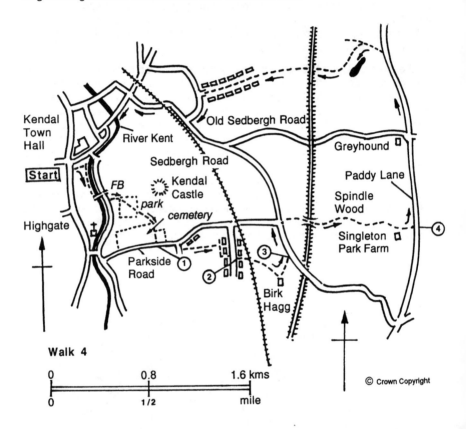

Walk 4

Start

From the Town Hall in Kendal cross the top of Lowther Street and go along Highgate for a few metres, then turn left down Yard 39, a narrow walled and cobbled ginnel running beside one of Kendal's famous snuff factories. At the bottom turn right for a few paces and enter a small private car park on the left, from where steps in the corner lead down to the riverside. Turn right, downstream, and cross the footbridge at Jennings Yard. Cross the main road and go up Parr Street on the far right-hand side. After crossing the humped backed bridge over the former Lancaster canal, fork diagonally right up a tarmac path through Fletcher Park, continuing through a kissing gate and over the shoulder of Castle Hill by a wall on the right to reach an enclosed path through the cemetery. Follow this path to Parkside Road (or go through the cemetery on the left - a riot of purple crocuses in March.)

1 Turn left along Parkside road. Just beyond the entrance to Archer's Meadow estate, opposite the cricket ground, a footpath starts on the right next to an electricity substation. It runs alongside a wall and goes uphill behind the older houses and over two stiles. At the top of the hill there is a fine view of Kendal Castle. Continue down to a stile leading into a walled path. Turn right, then left just past the second house to reach Valley Drive.

2 Cross Valley drive to the walled path 40 metres along the road to the right and follow this over the Oxenholme to Windermere branch railway, to reach a cart track going past Birk Hagg Farm and out to the Sedbergh road.

3 Turn left down the road for 350m to the first junction, then follow a narrow walled path on the right, signposted Spindle Woods and Paddy Lane, starting immediately to the right of a drive. Cross the stile at the top and continue along over a railway bridge, (the main line from Scotland to Euston this time) to reach a field by another stile beside a gate. Keep by the wall on the right to another gate with stile alongside, and then follow the beck, fording it just past a large oak tree. Now head up the hill towards an electricity pole, and keep by the hedge on the right to reach another gate and stile. Bear slightly left up the next field to a gate. The cleft hill over on the left is Benson Knott. Continue straight across the next two fields via a stile left of Singleton Park Farm to emerge onto Paddy Lane by a narrow gap stile.

4 Turn left along the lane for 700m to the crossroads, from where a short cut may be taken back to Kendal via the Old Sedbergh Road. Otherwise continue along Paddy Lane for about another 600m, mainly downhill, to a signpost and stile on the left. Cross the stile and follow the wall on the left to another gate and stile at the bottom of the field, crossing into a walled lane. After about 50m another stile will be found on the left. Go over this and take the well-used track straight ahead, descending gently through the rough heathland to another stile. From here the path crosses the bed of the former Lower Bird's Park reservoir, close to the line of the old dam, and rises up a steep bank at the far side (the remains of the old dam.) Here turn right, between fence and wall, to another stile on the left, then follow the wall on the left down to the main line railway, crossing under it by two stiles and a low tunnel. Keep by the wall on the right to join a cart track descending to the Sandylands estate, from where a bus may be taken to the town centre. Otherwise go straight down the road, Peat Lane, turn left at the bottom then right at the next T-junction, to reach the town centre at Stramongate Bridge over the Kent.

Sprint and Kent Circuit   9km (5.5miles)

The fast flowing River Kent and its tributaries, the Mint and Sprint, which join it just north of Kendal, hold many attractions for the walker at all seasons of the year. This walk includes two riverside paths, linked by a scenic high level fell road, with a few intricate field paths, muddy in places, to complete the circuit. Take the bus from Kendal to Burneside or park near Hall Park estate on the north-east side of the village, reached by turning right at the staggered crossroads (SD506959) in the centre of the village and passing the main entrance to Croppers paper mill.

Start
Follow the road out, using the fenced path on the left beyond the estate and continue past Burneside Hall, an old fortified farmhouse. Turn right at the road junction and continue straight ahead, past the left turn, to reach Sprint Bridge.

1   Cross the bridge and the stile on the left just beyond it, and then follow the river-bank to Sprint Mill. Cross a waymarked stile in front of you, and go up the bank to continue along and above the river. Just after passing the Thirlmere aqueduct, where it crosses the river in a pipe, the path continues left over a wooden stile in a fence and close by the riverbank past the converted mill buildings at Oak Bank. After another 400m you reach a footbridge over the old mill leat, at the end of a bank of trees on the right. Cross the bridge and then a stile, and leave the riverbank for a while, to head across the field towards a stile beside a gate. Cross the farm drive to another stile and bear left, up by the hedge to join a cart track going through a gate and over the hill. Aim just right of the trees across the next field to rejoin the riverbank, high above the water at this point. Follow the track, descending through trees, and look for a wooden stile and slab bridge on the left at the bottom of the bank, leading across a field to Gurnal Bridge. Cross the bridge and continue left up the road, for 150m, to find a stone step stile on the right. Go diagonally up the field to another stile just left of the barn. Cross the farm drive to a field gate opposite then go uphill to a ladder stile. Keep by the hedge on the right and between buildings to reach another road at Hill Farm.

2   Turn right along the road for about 150m to Hill Fold Farm on the left and go up past the house. Go through a gate on the left, into a large field, just before reaching the stock sheds. Go straight across the field to the far corner opposite, where you'll find a stile in the wall corner close to where it joins a fence. Beyond the stile keep by the wall on the left to a green lane. At the junction in the lane turn right for a few metres to a gate on the left, then head up the field towards the houses to cross the drive to Waterhouse by two metal stiles. Continue across another drive in the garden of the house to a small gate and then go round the curtilage of the buildings to another waymarked stile. After the stile aim half right, walking round a planted area in the paddock/orchard to a plank bridge and gate over a small beck. Now aim for the converted farm at Shepherd Green, crossing a wooden stile and going left of most of the buildings to reach the drive, and hence to the Potter Fell Road.

3   Turn left along the fell road with views of Kendal to the left and the Coniston fells ahead, on a clear day. Follow the road for about 1.5km until it drops down past High House Farm on the left, then the dormer-windowed Godmund Hall on the right. Just beyond the Hall follow the footpath sign on the right across the field to a stile. Cross a narrow drive to another stile and go down a small path by the beck to a footbridge. Cross and continue up the field towards a stile and some buildings. Turn right along the drive, going through a gate on the same line beyond the house. Follow the bridleway with the beck below on the right. At a three-way junction, near a large sycamore tree, follow the bridleway sign left to High Hundhowe through a gate. Pass the fine old barn with its stone water trough on the left and go down the drive to the road.

4   Turn right along the road for 150m, and just past the buildings follow the footpath sign on the left, going through the farmyard and down a rough track leading to the River Kent. Do not cross the bridge but go through the kissing gate on the left to follow the river bank past the vast new housing development at Cowan Head Mill. Go past Bowston Bridge and on along the riverbank to Burneside, reaching the road and the start of the walk by following the path round the edge of the paper mill site.

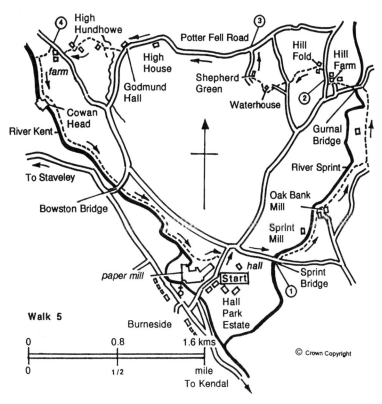

WALK No 6

Patton and Docker

9.6km (6miles)

This is an undulating walk through fields, with some quiet road walking. The route follows the Dalesway Long Distance footpath for about 2 miles. On a clear day there are fine views of the surrounding fells. This walk could be linked, near Grayrigg Foot with Walk No 10, thus making a walk of about 12.5miles. Park in the hamlet of Mealbank (SD541956). To reach this hamlet leave Kendal on the A6, passing under the railway bridge by Kendal station. In 1.6 mile turn right, signposted Mealbank. After several left and right bends the road follows the River Mint. Pass a right turn to a hump-backed bridge. Take the third turning to the right (next turning after a road called Laverock Hill, a modern estate) down into Laverock Mill industrial estate (Mealbank hamlet), where there is room to park.

Start

Walk back over the river to the Patton road. Turn left for 20m then follow the Footpath sign for Garnett Folds on the right, up a shallow valley, which is littered with Shap granite 'erratic' boulders brought down by the last ice sheet. Cross a stile over a wire fence and continue up the hill keeping just right of a small beck, to reach a corner where a wall meets a fence. Follow the fence/hedge on the left to the next stile, just beyond a gnarled ash tree. Keep straight ahead, and immediately after passing the ruins of Littlemire Farm turn sharp right uphill, to a gate at the top of the field. Beyond this, follow an old sunken track between ruined walls over the hill to reach a narrow lane.

1   Turn left up the lane for 30m, then go right, through two large field gates, then diagonally up the field to another gate in the far corner. Continue alongside the wall on the right, past an old quarry, and cross a wooden stile in a stopped-up gateway on the right, just before another gate. Now keep by the wall on the left as far as the ruins of 'Back of Patton' then bear right, aiming towards the buildings ahead to cross a ladder stile. Follow the wall on the left to a gate, then turn left through another gate and follow a cart track to New House. In front of the house turn right, up the hill beside the pylon. From the top of the hill there are fine views of the Silurian age Whinfell ridge with the Howgills further to the right. Immediately in front is Black Moss Tarn.

2   Descend to the left of the tarn, where you join the Dalesway, which is waymarked with yellow arrows for most of this section. Cross the first wall by a stile, then another stile at a bend in the next wall; cross the field to a third stile, and then follow the hedge on the right to reach Biglands via some narrow fields. Follow the drive to the road.

3   Cross the road and follow a rather overgrown track opposite that goes through two gates and into the garden of a converted barn (B&B). After passing a second barn conversion on the right, turn right along a track to a field gate. About 75m past the gate bear left through an old metal kissing gate onto the drive to Shaw End, a right of way at this point. Turn right along the drive for about 400m to a kissing

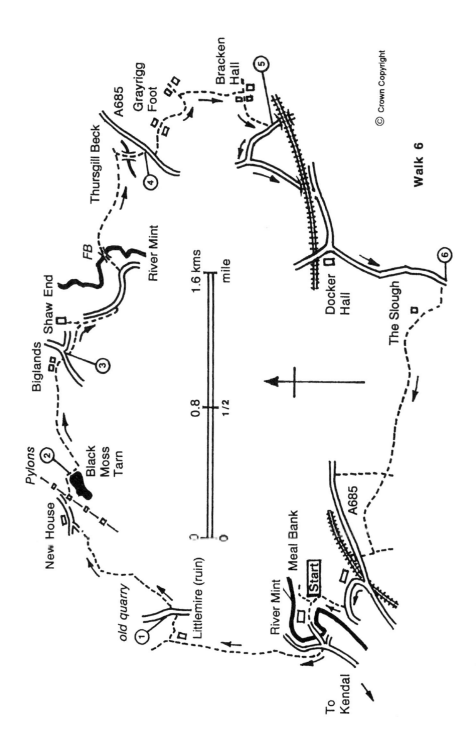

Walk 6

© Crown Copyright

Grayrigg Foot
A685
Bracken Hall
Thursgill Beck
⑤
④
River Mint
FB
Shaw End
Biglands
③
Docker Hall
Pylons
②
Black Moss Tarn
New House
The Slough
old quarry
①
Littlemire (ruin)
⑥
River Mint
Meal Bank
Start
A685
To Kendal

1.6 kms
0.8
0
mile
1/2

15

gate on the left, and then go down the field to the footbridge over the River Mint. Cross the bridge and bear right uphill and across the field to a field gate. Pass through this gate to a track ahead and then a path with a hedge on the right. Cross the waymarked stiles and drop down to the bridge over Thursgill Beck, then follow the farm drive right, uphill to the main road.

4   Turn right along the A685 for 80m then turn left up the drive to Grayrigg Foot Farm.   Pass through between the buildings, over the footbridge and through the gate, keeping by a hedged stream on the right.   After 90m, curve left to reach the drive to Greenhead.   Before reaching a bungalow, turn right to a gate near the corner of the field, leaving the Dalesway at this point. Keep straight ahead over the hill, to the right of a large oak tree, to reach a gate into the next field, then bear right, aiming for a solitary large sycamore tree and Bracken Hall beyond.   Cross a stile leading between the buildings, and then turn right, just beyond the house, to follow the farm drive to the road.

5   Turn right, and at the next minor road turn sharply left, following up Flodder Beck, to pass under the impressive six arched limestone mainline railway viaduct (1846). Soon, turn right for 300m on the road, as far as the next junction (ignoring a drive on the left to Tenter End). Turn left onto Docker Lane. About 120m after going under the supergrid power line go right, through a gate (signed Mealbank).

6   Head diagonally right towards a small footbridge near the wall, and beyond it a wicket gate.   Cross into the next field, and keeping above the beck, go round the outside of the top paddock wall at the Slough, then keep straight on towards a facing wall.   Turn left along the wall, where a waymark points towards a stile with a stream and footbridge beyond.   Cross the beck and go straight up the steep bank through the trees and across the field, right of some small old quarries, to cross a wooden step stile into the next field. Keep going ahead, aiming between two large trees, to reach a gate. Follow the track slightly downhill, passing about 20m right of a waterworks building, and then crossing a ruined wall and a small stream and going through sparse woodland to find a stone gap stile in the next wall, just right of a larch tree. Keep on in the same direction, slightly downhill, and cross the next wall by a step stile.   Now keep along the contours to enter a stony walled track just below a stone barn, and from here descend to the A685, close by the former tollhouse on the Kendal to Appleby turnpike. Turn left along the road for 200m to 'Mealbank Top' (bus stop), and go down the lane to Mealbank. Ignore the footpath sign on the right but turn right onto an unmade road at the next junction, back to the industrial estate.

Underbarrow and Lord's Lot   9.6km (6miles)

This walk is entirely within the Lake District National Park and visits the scattered villages of Underbarrow and Crosthwaite, and some rough upland pastures, including Lord's Lot, from where fine views can be obtained. The walk is unsuitable in misty conditions, as distant landmarks are necessary for navigation. Park the car near Underbarrow Church, at SD463926.

Start

Turn right, down the road past the old school, and cross a stile on the left just beyond the bridge, keeping straight ahead to a small gate into a field. Turn right and follow the hedge along to a wall stile where the hedge ends. Over the stile follow the hedge on the left to another stile, then aim towards the buildings ahead (The Broom), to cross a high ladder stile. Continue to a gate, then turn right, through the drive of the house and out onto a metalled road. There are noisy, boisterous dogs here, but their bark is worse than their bite!

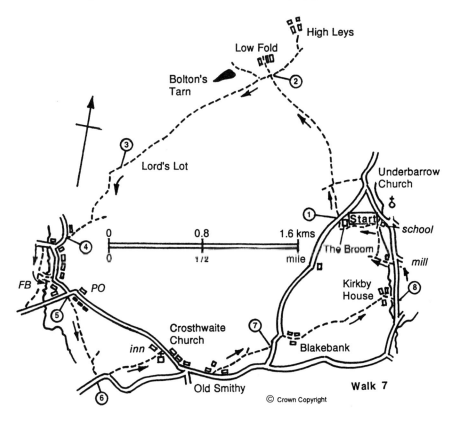

© Crown Copyright

Walk 7

17

1   Go straight across the lane and up a rough track opposite to a stile and gate. Keep by the wall on the left for about 250m, until a second gate gives access to a walled track. Turn right and go downhill, for about 50m to a wooden stile on the left at the corner of a wood. Now go up the steep bank ahead, following waymarks and keeping roughly parallel to the boundary of the wood on the right. At the top of the hill there are fine views, both behind, of the Lyth valley, the Kent estuary and Arnside Knott, and ahead, northwards to the Kentmere Fells. The view ahead includes two farms - aim for the left-hand one, Low Fold, following the line of the walls on the left until you reach a conspicuous ladder stile after about 400m from the brow of the hill. Cross the stile and keep by the wall on the right to another stile and then onto a cart track leading to a crossways about 100m short of Low Fold.

2   Turn left, and shortly bear half left, leaving the track for another ladder stile that leads to open pasture again. Keep straight ahead between the hills - the hill on the right conceals Bolton's Tarn, now overgrown but still a fine habitat for wetland species. Eventually you reach a cross wall with a wooden stile (not the gate) leading into Lord's Lot itself. The path runs beside the wall on the right, but a diversion to the higher ground on the left avoids boggy areas. Soon a clear, well-used track appears, muddy in places. Follow this downhill between the gorse bushes and across the long sloping pasture to reach a wooden stile next to a field gate where a wall meets a fence.

3   Cross the stile and bear left along a rough cart track for 150m. When you see the first mature oak tree on the right, with a stone outcrop under it, leave the track and go to the right of this tree, descending gently, to reach a wet hollow where another cart track joins your route from the right. Some hawthorn bushes here mark the corner of an old field boundary. The right of way continues to the right of the line of old hawthorns, but as this is overgrown it is easier to keep to the left of them in the open pasture. Eventually the faint path reaches an iron gate into a walled lane. Follow this lane right, to the road.

4   Turn left along the road and right at the T-junction, signposted to Hubbersty Head. Cross the bridge and the stile on the left just beyond it, then follow the fence on the right over the hill and down to another stile. Now bear left over wet ground, to a wooden kissing gate leading to an interesting old clapper bridge, and so to the road again. Turn right for about 300m to Crosthwaite Green, and a major road. There is a village shop a little way left up the road from here.

5   Cross the major road and follow the footpath sign between the houses opposite, down a bank to a stile and field. Cross the field to the stile opposite, and keep going in the same direction through various stiles and wall gaps, first with the wall on the right, then on the left, and then on the right again. Eventually you descend to a stile and gate in the corner of the last field, giving access to a farm road. Follow this unmetalled road right for about 200m to a metalled road.

6   Turn left up the road for 50m and go up a well-maintained bridleway that crosses the shoulder of Church Bank and leads directly to Crosthwaite Church. Go straight through the churchyard, passing the church door, and out through a stile

and up a path behind the Punch Bowl Inn to the main road. Turn right along the road towards Kendal for about 500m, then go diagonally left up an unmade road with cottages, starting by the old smithy, which, though hardly picturesque, still fulfils a useful function. Beyond the cottages the road becomes a cart track and some 30m before it takes a left-hand bend, go through a low stone stile on the right. Go diagonally over the shoulder of the hill to reach a gate onto a metalled byroad.

7   Turn left and after about 100m go right, down the drive to Middle Blakebank. The right of way passes immediately in front of the house and down a broad grassy path to a gate at the bottom of the garden. Continue beside the wall/hedge on the left, keeping to the top of a spur, until you drop down into a walled track and reach a bridge over a small beck. Bear left to a stile, and then follow the wall on the right to another stile, from where you follow the bottom of a bank towards the modern barn ahead. Enter the farmyard of Kirkby House Farm by a stile at the left-hand end of the barn, and go through between the buildings and out along the drive, over Chapel Beck, to the road.

8   Turn left along the road for 300m and then turn left down a yard (with large trucks) to the old water mill buildings, sadly now showing few signs of their former use. Go round behind the left of the buildings and up to a gate. Ahead is a really fine specimen of an oak tree, growing from an outcrop. Go up the bank and round the far side of the tree to see it to best advantage then drop down to the beck. Shortly you will see a small clapper bridge crossing this beck, which presumably served as a leat for the water mill. Cross here and continue along by the beck to reach the small gate used just after starting the walk.

Underbarrow Church

19

WALK NO. 8

Winster Valley 1   **10.4km (6.5miles)**

The beautiful unspoilt Winster Valley in the Lake District National Park is a veritable paradise for walkers, with its well-marked paths, its craggy woodlands, bracken-covered slopes and undulating pastures. This walk and the next one can be combined to make a 13 mile walk by using a short link path at Winster House; either of two excellent inns at Bowland bridge would then make an ideal half way refreshment point. However, it is inadvisable to follow the second of these walks in early summer before the grass is cut, both because of possible damage to the crop, and also for your own comfort, particularly in wet weather. It is possible to park a car in a lay-by on the right side of the B5284 Kendal to Bowness Road, about 1mile beyond the entrance to Windermere Golf Club, and about 100m before reaching the entrance to the Linthwaite House Hotel. G.R.   SD 407957

Start

Follow the signposted path that begins close to the drive to the hotel. A permissive path takes you between gardens, but the right of way goes straight ahead to meet the drive to the hotel. Continue on an enclosed path alongside the drive, beside ornamental duck ponds. On reaching a wooden kissing gate go diagonally up the field, through a clump of trees, over the hill and down to the right-hand of two gates seen ahead. Follow the telephone line to the gate by the house, and continue past the end of the house and down a rough path to a steep stile in a wall, leading to the drive of Lindeth Farm.

1   Turn right along the drive and go through the farmyard to a waymarked gate, then follow a good track across two fields to reach a walled drive to a house. Pass the house on your right and follow the waymark on the electricity pole beyond, to reach a gate into a rough pasture - this is where the return route meets the outward route, (Z on map).   Just past the gate go down some rough steps next to the wall on the right and continue by the wall to an iron kissing gate. Through the gate follow the path and cross a drive to reach a wooden kissing gate, then bear left along a rough green track as it snakes between many stone outcrops and eventually reaches the Bowness to Levens Bridge road (A5074).

2   Turn right along the road for about l00m to the entrance to Barker Knott Farm with its interesting old buildings. Go through the farmyard and out on a stony track via an iron gate. When this track bears left, uphill, leave it and follow the wall on the right, with a large tarn to be seen over the wall. Keep by the wall almost to the next farm, Bellman Ground, but just before the buildings turn left up a modern fenced and metalled drive, and follow it for about 700m, as far as Rosthwaite Farm. Go through the left-hand of two formidable modern gateways and follow the drive round to the left of all the buildings, and past a large pond, eventually to reach a gateway leading to an old and rough track just past the riding school. Follow this track across rough pasture for 500m to where, near the top of a hill a signpost points left to Ghyll Head. (A short detour to the right leads to an excellent viewpoint over Windermere). Follow the path left to a stile and continue by the side of a wood to a wooden kissing gate. Then take the diversion through the Ghyll Head Access

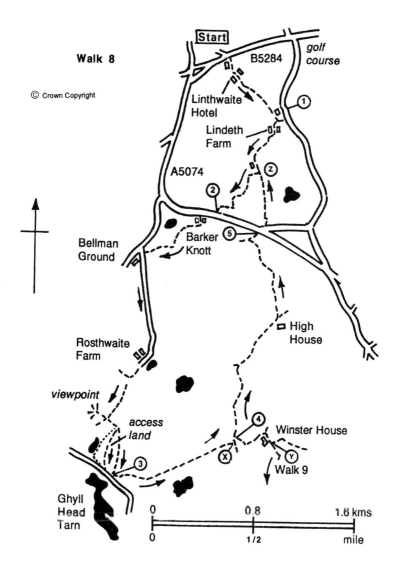

Walk 8

© Crown Copyright

Start

B5284

golf course

Linthwaite Hotel

Lindeth Farm

A5074

Bellman Ground

Barker Knott

High House

Rosthwaite Farm

viewpoint

access land

Winster House

Walk 9

Ghyll Head Tarn

0   0.8   1.8 kms

0   1/2   mile

Area, an attractive piece of land owned by the National Park Authority, to emerge onto the Ghyll Head road. Across the road is Ghyll Head Reservoir, used for fishing.

3   Continue by following the signposted path towards Winster, which bears right in front of the next kissing gate and continues across rough open pasture (planted with trees in 1998) for about 1km, eventually to reach a stony track going along beside a wall. At this point (X on the map), the link can be made with Winster Valley

2 (Walk No. 9). To do this go through the gate in the wall and continue down a walled lane for 350m, through a gate, and bear right on a metalled drive past some converted outbuildings and Winster House (mentioned in para 5 of Walk No 9).

4   To complete Walk No 8, turn left along the stony track beside the wall and follow it for about 1km, as it gradually descends towards High House. Where the track turns right, into the farmyard ("no access" notice), ignore the field gate straight ahead, and bear left alongside the wall to go through two gates. Continue, hugging the wall on the right for 600m, eventually to reach a green lane going right to meet the A5074 road again.

5   Cross the road and go up the track opposite for a few metres until reaching a signposted stone stile in the wall on the left. Go under the power lines and round to the left of the rocky hill in front, then continue climbing and following the power lines to reach a gate leading via more rough pasture to the junction with the outward route at another gate (Z on map). Go through the gate and follow the outward route, via Lindeth Farm, back to the start.

BARKER KNOTT FARM.
WINSTER VALLEY.

P. Standish

Winster Valley 2 11.2km (7 miles)

Winster Valley 2   **11.2km (7 miles)**

This walk and the previous one may be combined to make a longer walk of about 13 miles by using a short link path near Winster House (see paragraph 5). The start and finish of Walk No 8 should then be omitted (see map). The remarks in the introduction to walk No 8 about the Winster valley also apply to this walk. It is however inadvisable to follow this walk in early summer before the grass is cut, because of possible damage to the crop and also for your own comfort, particularly in wet weather. Start the walk at Bowland Bridge on the pre-1800 turnpike road between Kendal and Newby Bridge (SD418896). There is parking space near the telephone kiosk.

Start

Take the road signposted to Witherslack and Grange, beside the Hare and Hounds and after l00m cross a stile on the left near an electricity pole. Keep by the wall on the right across the first two fields, then cross a corner stile and stay by the wall, which is now on your left. On reaching open pasture keep straight ahead, left of the power line, to pass left of a barn, and continue to a stile onto a byroad.

1   Cross the road slightly left to a signposted path through large metal gates. Cross the field to join a cart track. After going through the gate into the third field, bear half left to a stile in the left-hand wall. Go over the stile and straight across the field to a gate opposite, beyond a small beck. Bear right through the gateway and follow the left-hand side of the wall/hedge over the top of the hill, through two stiles and down to a gate at the bottom of the third field. From the gate bear right to follow the wall to a stile onto a minor road. Cross the road by the two stiles, following the wall on the left to a third stile. Now keep straight ahead reaching the A5074 at another stile.

2   Turn right along the road to another signposted stile on the left, crossing this to reach Low Yews through a gate to the orchard. Turn right here, in front of the cottages and go through a waymarked field gate on the left at the end of the buildings. Follow the wall down to another gate, then cross this field to another waymarked field gate. Now follow the hedge on the left to a stile in the far corner of the field, go through and turn right to follow the hedge which is now on your right. After crossing the next stile, keep by the hedge on the right to another stile, and on across the field to a stile leading onto the drive at Mearsons, near Hubbersty Head. Cross the drive and the mown grass to another wall stile onto a minor road.

3   Turn right up the road and after about 300m turn left at a footpath sign and go up a stony track through a small wood, to a stile in the corner, leading into a field. Keep by the left-hand boundary, crossing two ladder stiles, after which go down by the wall on the right, past a spring, to a gate in the wall leading to two wooden stiles crossing a concrete drive. Now keep straight ahead by the plantation on the right to reach a stile onto another road in the far corner of the field.

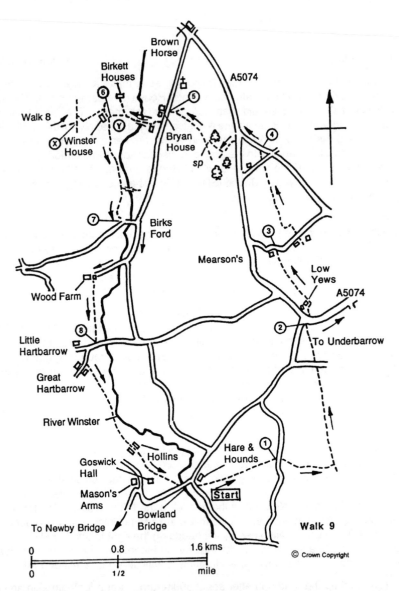

Brown Horse

Birkett Houses

A5074

⑥

Walk 8

Ⓨ

⑤

Ⓧ Winster House

Bryan House

sp

④

⑦

Birks Ford

Mearson's

③

Low Yews

A5074

Wood Farm

②

To Underbarrow

Little Hartbarrow

⑧

Great Hartbarrow

River Winster

Goswick Hall

Hollins

Hare & Hounds

①

Mason's Arms

Start

To Newby Bridge

Bowland Bridge

Walk 9

© Crown Copyright

0   0.8   1.6 kms

0   1/2   mile

4   Turn left along the byroad to reach the A5074 again, then turn left on the main road for about 100m to a signposted footpath on the right in a lay-by. Over the stile bear left, towards the wood, crossing a small stream and boggy ground to reach a gate and bridge in the bottom corner. Now bear half right, to go up the steep slope between the trees. A waymark near the top points left as the old track zigzags up

the slope. You soon come to a three-way signpost, where you turn sharp right again to go between two freestanding gateposts onto a stony track. Follow this track as it curves round below the trees on the left, continuing for a further 500m or so to reach a road at Bryan House Farm. Winster Church lies just to the north.

5   Turn left on the road past Bryan House Farm and in about l00m turn right down the signposted drive to Winster House. Ignoring the drive to Birkett House, keep straight ahead, and after turning a right-hand bend near some rhododendrons, go through a gap on the left onto a grassy track going sharp back to the left. At this point (Y on the map) you can join Winster Valley 1 (Walk No 8). If you wish to do this, continue past Winster House and follow the metalled drive round to the left past the converted outbuildings, through a gate, uphill on a grassy track between walls, to reach the stony track mentioned in paragraph 3 of Winster Valley 1 (Walk No 8)

6   To continue the Winster Valley 2 walk follow the grassy track you reached just before Winster House and keep a hedge, then a wall on your left before reaching open fields above the River Winster. Keep by the 'river' across the next fields to join a track coming down from the right near an old kiln, (This was once used for burning green bracken to make potash, used in the production of lye for washing fleeces). Continuing in the same direction, follow this track along the field, ignoring a footbridge on the left, to reach a minor road via a track through the wood on the right. Turn left down the road to reach Birks Ford and its old stone clapper bridge.

7   Cross the bridge and turn right along the road for 400m, then turn right into the drive to Wood Farm. On reaching the buildings before the house go round the left-hand end of the barn and follow a green lane with an old orchard on the right. Leave the lane at the waymarked gate, part way along on the left, and cross two fields. Bear slightly right, uphill, to a gate in the far upper corner of the second field, near a wood. Continue along the contours to reach another byroad by a track through a small wood.

8   Turn right up the road for about 500m to a signpost to Hollins Farm on the left, just below Great Hartbarrow Farm. Cross two short fields and go through the left-hand of two gateways at the end of the second field, just beyond a small clapper bridge. Cross the next field to a gate at the far side. Now follow the wall on the left and go into a walled lane leading to Hollins Farm. Go through the gate and pass immediately in front of the house, (past an old cheese press on the right). Keep on up the drive, and just beyond the end of the garden go through a small gate on the left leading via a permissive path into the next field. Turn right in the field and keep by the wall to a gate. Cross to a stile near the middle of the next hedge to reach a field near Goswick Hall. Now aim for a waymark near a hawthorn tree, and then keep by the wall on the right to reach a waymarked stone stile in the corner of a wood. Continue to a kissing gate in a wire fence and on through the wood to emerge into a field near a large oak tree. Cross the field diagonally left to reach a stile onto the road near Bowland Bridge and the starting point.

Under Whinfell   11.2km (7miles)

This unspoilt part of Kendal's local countryside is dominated at every point by views of Whinfell Beacon, as the route circles round the village of Grayrigg. The ruins of two cairns can just be seen on the summit of the fell. They date from the 15th Century and fires were lit here to warn of oncoming Scottish invaders. A. W. Wainwright, the famous Lakeland author, tells us that the remaining trees near the summit were part of a wood planted to supply timber for the fires. Park on the verge of the A685 Kendal to Tebay road, at SD571970. This lies between the entrance to 'Kapellan' (the animal shelter set up by A. W. Wainwright and his second wife) and the drive to Ghyll Bank, marked by a white signpost. You may prefer to park at the far end of the village of Grayrigg and start the walk where it crosses the main road (ie. at paragraph 5). The walk could also be linked with Walk No 6, near Grayrigg Foot, thus making a walk of 12.5miles.

Start
Walk up the road towards Tebay and, after a few metres, turn left and follow the right-hand drive past Ghyll Bank and through a gate at the end of the yard, to descend into a delightful secluded valley. Follow the track through a gate past the converted buildings of Bye Mill, with the old mill leat up on your right. Cross a footbridge over the beck 250m beyond the buildings. Continue alongside another minor stream on the left, with a hedge coming in on the right after 100m, until a gate is reached. Continue through the gate and up a rise ahead to reach another gate with a road beyond.

1   Turn left along the road for about 700m, with fine views of Whinfell Beacon over on the right, past the drives of High and Low Deepslack farms, to reach a crossroads. Turn left here along a farm drive. After 350m, go through a field gate on the right as the track bends left. Go about 50m down an old sunken grass track then turn sharp right along a line of old tree stumps. After passing a solitary ash tree, keep in the same direction across wet ground to a small iron gate leading into the corner of a field on the left. Climb diagonally up the bank, bearing left to reach Stone Hall through a field gate. Pass in front of the house through two more gates and out on the drive to a further gate onto a lane.

2   Turn left along this lane as far as the next buildings on the right - Chapel House, a former Methodist chapel, and the Old School House. Go through a small iron gate just beyond the schoolhouse and along a grassy path between low garden walls to reach a hedged path behind the buildings. This leads into a field, with a view of Whinfell Tarn ahead. Go down the field by the hedge to a stile at the bottom and cross over the lane and through a gate into another field. Bear half right, to pass the end of the tarn and cross the field to reach a wooden stile in the middle of the far fence. Continue in the same direction to a gate into a farm drive in the far corner of the next field. Turn right along the drive to reach Topthorn Farm. Go up the yard and cross diagonally in front of the house to leave by a gate or gates into a green lane. Continue on the lane until it opens out into a field, then continue towards a

gateway at the bottom of the field, with Whinfell Beacon directly in line. Keep along the lower part of the next field with a wire fence on the left. Cross a wall stile at the far end, then go up half right to a gate or stile in the wall corner leading into a lane.

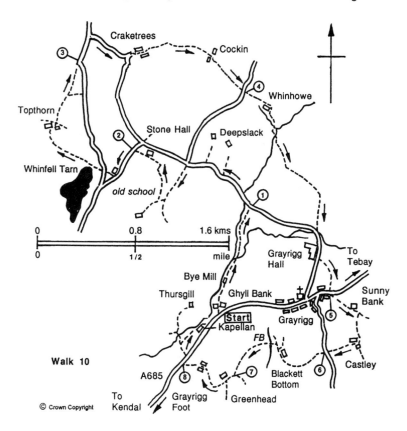

3   Go left up the lane as far as the next junction, and then turn right for 450m to reach the entrance to Crakelrees, (signed Whinfell Nurseries on a plaque in the wall) on a corner. Go up the drive past the house and some sheds and follow the track left to a field gate and stile. Aim to the right of the derelict barn across the field and go through a gate in the far corner near a large sycamore tree. Go ahead up the next field by the hedge, straight on over a drive and down to a gate in the next wall. Continue by the wall on the left to reach Cockin Farm. Pass between the farmhouse and the barn then turn right through a gate behind the barn. Pass through a second gate then keep up the left of the field by a wire fence to another gate. Go down the following field to a step stile into a small wood next to a drinking trough, and straight through the wood onto the metalled road that leads up to the repeater station on Whinfell ridge.

4   Cross straight over the unfenced road and through the field to a wall stile in the far right corner. Cross another field to a gate, before descending to a large barn at Whinhowe. Go round the far end of the barn and out onto a farm track via a gate. After crossing over a small beck on the track, head off left, down to a footbridge over Whinhowe Gill, the same beck you followed near the start of the walk. Cross this beck and stay by the fence at first, then head diagonally across the field and over a wall stile marked by a wooden post opposite. Keep right of the old quarry, and then head half left to a gate that can be seen on the hill. From here a cart track soon becomes a concrete drive leading to Grayrigg Hall Farm, seen ahead with Grayrigg Church behind. On reaching the farm go through a small wooden gate opposite the farmhouse. Head diagonally across the field and round the left of the hill ahead, then go up to the main road (A685), joining it at a step stile a few metres left of the old terraced cottages.

5   Cross the main road carefully and go left for a short way to a footpath sign on the right, leading up beside some gardens. Continue to follow this waymarked path to Sunny Bank, the next farm. Pass through the farmyard and after the buildings, bear right off the main track and down a field, aiming for Castley Bank Farm seen ahead. Bear right into the farmyard, going through two gates and out past the farmhouse onto the drive. Follow the drive to the lane.

6   Cross the lane and go through a gate into a field. Go down the field to a small beck that leads to a waymarked gate at the bottom. Continue by the beck on an old cart track to Blackett Bottom. Go through two gates, passing the first group of houses and along the drive to another gate. Immediately after, head left, down the bank, and over the beck by a footbridge. Go straight ahead over the shoulder of the hill to a field gate, then veer left along the contours across the next field and through another gate. Turn left, up by the hedge, veering right towards the end of the field to go through a gateway near the outbuildings of Greenhead Farm. After the gate look left for a stile out onto a green lane, often hidden by silage bales. You are now on the Dalesway long distance path for the next 700m.

7   Turn right along the farm lane and down the drive, and on nearing the cattle grid at the bottom of the field, bear right along an old terraced track that leads to a gate near a footbridge over a beck. Cross the bridge and go through Grayrigg Foot Farm and out on its drive to the main road again.

8   Turn right for 50m along the road. Turn left up the drive to Thursgill then descend to the corner of a wood, where a caravan offers refreshments to thirsty Dalesway walkers if they are lucky. Here you leave the Dalesway and follow a narrow path starting behind the caravan and climbing obliquely up, through a splendid bluebell wood in spring. Go through a small gate onto an enclosed path behind the animal shelter at 'Kapellan'. You may not see any animals but you will certainly hear them heralding your approach. Through another small gate steps lead down behind the garage, above a steep drop, to emerge through an opening into the visitor's car park. (Visits are by appointment only.) Turn left at the road, and walk about 100m to the starting point.

Walk No. 11

Drumlin Country   12km (7.5miles)

The undulating nature of the country through which this walk passes is the result of the many drumlins, rounded hummocks of boulder clay which were carried down from the north and shaped by ice during the last ice age over ten thousand years ago. The ridges of the drumlins provide some good distant views, while the former Lancaster to Kendal canal, open to navigation from 1819 to 1955, lends interest to an area split by the intrusion of the A591 trunk road. This was built in 1974 as a link from the M6 to Kendal and the Lake District. The walk is perhaps best avoided in the height of summer as there are lots of fields with long grass (for silage) and some paths are liable to be overgrown with nettles; however, there are no muddy farmyards on the route. There is space for parking by the roadside at Leasgill (SD496840) just off the A6 between Levens Bridge and Milnthorpe, but the road will be crowded with cars at school opening and closing times. The Kendal to Milnthorpe bus stops by the village Hall.

Start
About 50m north of the village hall, a flight of concrete steps leads up to a side road (not the cul-de-sac near the bus stop). Follow the side road uphill for about 400m to find a stone gap stile on the left (signpost obscured). Go through the avenue of sycamore trees to reach a bridleway beyond, and then turn left for 70m before turning right at a signpost indicating Hincaster and Levens Bridge. Traverse along the slope with a wood, and later a wall, on the right, to reach High Barns Farm. Immediately before the farmhouse climb a high stone step stile and keep by the hedge on the left to reach a cart track near the cowshed. Continue in the same direction, following the track over the hill to reach Hincaster Hall Farm. This fine building dates from the 16th Century and is a good example of a local traditional farmhouse with its mullioned windows and round chimneys. Continue down the metalled farm drive to the road.

DRUMLINS NEAR THE LANCASTER CANAL   M.Adams

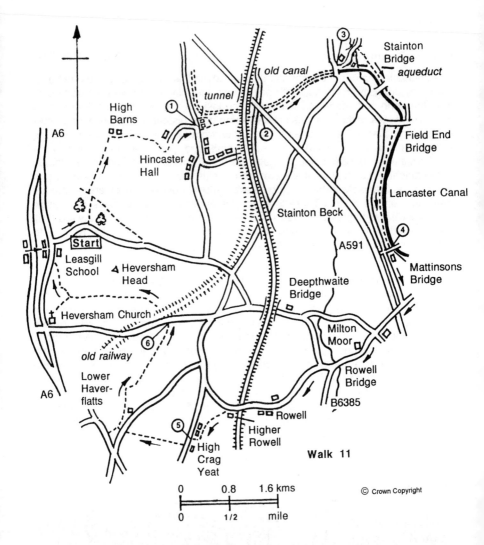

Walk 11

```
0        0.8      1.6 kms
├────┼────┼────┤
0        1/2      mile
```

© Crown Copyright

1   The route continues up the signposted bridleway opposite, but a short detour as far as the end of the houses on the left is worthwhile to inspect the entrance to the canal tunnel. The tunnel took the Lancaster canal some 350m under the drumlinoid Tunnel Hill, while the barge horses were led over the top along the bridleway. To regain the route take the horse path on the right in front of the tunnel entrance and behind the cottages, to join the bridleway as it goes left between hedges and over the top of the hill. The bridleway and tunnel have been declared an ancient monument. Follow the path under the mainline railway and down to the road.

2   Turn left, and then right after passing under the A591 to rejoin the sunken remains of the canal. Follow the towpath as far as the second bridge, where the canal still retains water.

3   The route lies south, and the main towpath can be used, but a more interesting way, possibly rather overgrown in summer, is to cross the bridge then turn right, into the southern part of the hamlet of Stainton, and continue as far as the bridge over Stainton Beck. (A detour between the cottages on the right before reaching the bridge will give you a view of the small aqueduct that carries the canal over Stainton Beck). Just beyond the bridge cross a stile on the right, and go right, by the edge of the field to reach another stile that leads to the canal embankment on the opposite side from the main towpath. Continue on the bank, past the next bridge and a further 210m to join Commonmire Lane by going down a steep path on the left through the trees, 150m before Field End Bridge. Follow the lane to the bridge and cross the canal to rejoin the main towpath via a slope on the left. Continue south along the towpath for about 1km to reach Mattinson's Bridge where a right turn up some steps then down a grassy track leads past a cottage to the road (Note that this track is not a right of way, but the occupier has allowed permissive access. Please be sure to shut the gate!)

4   Turn left along this minor road, unfortunately marred by the noise from the adjacent trunk road. At the junction turn right on the B6385. Cross over the trunk road where a glance back will reveal an imposing row of drumlins. Continue along the B road for another 700m. past Milton Moor Farm to Rowell Bridge then bear right, up a minor road, keeping straight ahead at the next junction. After about 1km on this minor road, beyond the railway and just past Higher Rowell Farm, follow a signpost on the left through the left-hand of two gates. Keep by the hedge on the right, then cross the middle of the next field, and just past the bungalows on the right, cross a stile into a hedged path (possibly overgrown in summertime) leading to the road.

5   Turn left for l00m to the footpath sign opposite High Cragg Yeat. Go straight across the field to a gate then up the hedge on the left to a stile, continuing to a narrow slate stile on the crest of this drumlin. Descend to another stile and cross a narrow lane to a third. Now aim for the field gate about two thirds of the way down the field, go through and then contour along the next field to the left of the converted buildings (Lower Haverflatts) to reach a gate at the far right-hand corner. Keep by the hedge along the next field, and then go right, round the edge of the third field to a stile in the far right corner. From here the route descends, to the right of a lone tree to a stile opposite the right-hand end of the tree belt ahead.

6   Turn left along the road and almost immediately turn right through a gateway, to cross the dismantled Arnside to Hincaster railway and reach the playing fields of Dallam School. Bear slightly left to a stile in the curved wall across the playing field, and then go diagonally up the slope, aiming right of a clump of trees. Keep above the trees to a second clump, then contour round the hill, with fine views of the Kent estuary, descending towards the left side of the wood ahead. From here a kissing gate gives access to a track through the wood, leading to Leasgill, and the start of the walk.

Birkbeck Fells and Bretherdale   15 km (8 miles)

This walk and the following one almost join at Bretherdale Head and the two can be combined to make a figure of eight walk of up to 18 miles. This walk crosses Birkbeck Fells, a moorland area of grass and heather with wide views to the east, then descends to the hamlet of Greenholme. The return route visits the lovely remote valley of Bretherdale. Do choose a clear day, and wear boots, as parts of the walk are very wet underfoot. Don't be put off by the boring start to the walk - it's worth it! Travel north up the A6 from Kendal for 10 miles and leave the car (or the Shap bus?) at the first layby on the left before you reach the summit of the hill after climbing from Huck's Bridge. There is a stile and gate in the fence on the right where the walk finishes. (NY554059)

Start
Walk north up the road for about 1km, passing the telephone kiosk and going under one set of power lines, then cross a stile on the right beside a gate and follow a good gravel track for a further 1km. The prominent overhead wires will soon be left behind. As you approach a forestry plantation and a gate ahead, go through a gate on the right onto another hard track and follow it across the moor. Ignore the left fork leading to a shooting hut and keep to the main track until its end just past its highest point and near a white gas marker post.

1   A rougher track now commences, going left past the summit of Crag Hill (with a cairn). A detour to the cairn will give a good view of the route ahead towards Tebay, and the ruined barn that is the next objective. Follow the faintly sunken old bridleway, ignoring any modern vehicular tracks, as it snakes round and eventually reaches the ruined barn at Nan Hill. Just beyond the barn, near a low erratic boulder, leave the line of the main track and go half right down the slope, aiming just left of the mature pine trees in the valley bottom. Soon you will find another faint track that goes above the ruined farmhouse at Eskew Head. On reaching a wall, drop down beside it and go through a gateway in the wall, leading to a barn. Go through the gap above the barn, then contour across the next two fields above the marshes, ignoring a cart track cutting across diagonally, and keeping above the crags, to reach a wire fence with a stile at the intersection of another fence. Cross the stile and continue to the converted farmhouse at Low Crag. Pass left round the buildings to find a stone stile in the wall corner at the end of the garden. Contour across the field; go through a gate then downhill to a wooden stile at the wall/fence junction. Follow the wall down to a gate and then through to a metalled lane at Eskew Beck House. (A short cut is possible here by following the road to the right for 750m to rejoin the main route where it crosses the road at the top of the hill. If doing this omit the next two paragraphs.)

2   Turn left and follow the road for 220m to a footpath sign pointing down right to a stile at the wall corner near the small beck. Cross this stile and another one ahead, then follow the wall and beck on the right to a narrow gate at the bottom of the field. Cross the beck beyond the gate and follow it down through gorse bushes,

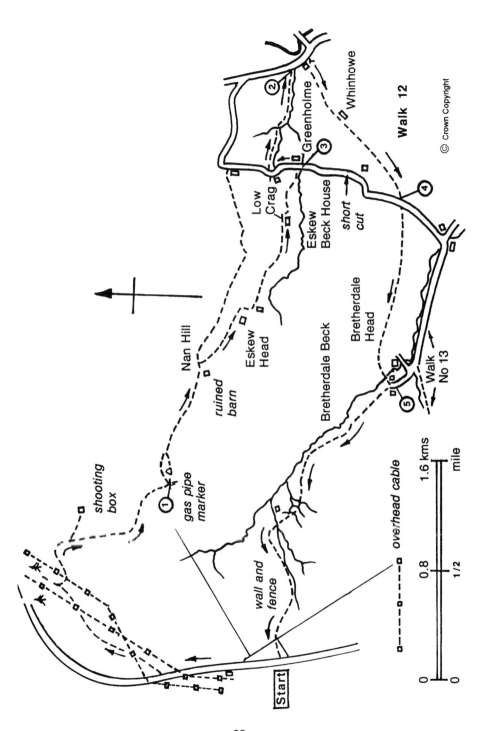

Walk 12

© Crown Copyright

Whinhowe

Greenholme

Low
Crag

Eskew
Beck House

short
cut

Nan Hill

Bretherdale
Head

Eskew
Head

ruined
barn

Bretherdale Beck

Walk
No 13

shooting
box

gas pipe
marker

wall and
fence

overhead cable

Start

| 0 | 0.8 | 1.6 kms |
| 0 | 1/2 | mile |

33

crossing another stile and a second stile in the corner of the wall to approach Greenholme Farm. Just before the farm cross a footbridge over the beck leading to a stile that brings you to the centre of the hamlet of Greenholme.

3   Continue to the telephone kiosk and turn right just beyond it up a track leading to Low Whinhowe, a half-ruined farmstead. Continue on through the farmyard but leave the track at a small ruined outbuilding and go straight ahead up a sunken track beside a wire fence. The sunken track is fairly clear on the ground and continues across several fields in the same direction, climbing gently for about 700m distance. It then descends slightly to join an unfenced metalled road near the top of a hill. From here you can see down into the valley of Bretherdale, which curves away to the right out of sight.

4   Cross the road and continue along the track that runs at high level on the north side of the valley for 1km. Eventually the track descends towards Bretherdale Head Farm and you cross Bretherdale Beck by its curious stone footbridge. (At this point a 200m link to Walk No 13 is possible by going straight ahead between the half-ruined buildings and down the track as far as the junction with the Breasthigh track coming over from Borrowdale.)

5   After crossing the footbridge go right, alongside the beck, passing between the beck and the next ruined building. Keep following the faint track, bearing left round a hill when approaching a ruined wall, and going through a gate in a wire fence. The track continues, climbing gradually up the valley above the beck and crossing some very wet patches of ground, for another 600m until reaching another ruined wall. Don't go through the gateway, but follow the line of the sunken track up beside the wall. Continue along the contours above the wall, crossing three more tributaries of the main beck before the wall veers off right. Now cross some open ground at the same level, still on a faint track, to reach a ford at the junction of two more tributaries. After this keep ahead up the line of rubble that marks the edge of the track. After the end of the stones the track curves to the left, but it disappears, to reappear 20m higher up the fell, going diagonally up the slope to the left. Keep climbing gently, parallel to the small beck on the left, aiming for the dip on the skyline. When you reach a ditch draining into the nearby beck turn 45 degrees right and aim for the highest ground ahead, to reach a wall just over the summit. Follow the wall right to a stile and gate. This leads across heather to the stile and gate seen by the A6 at the start of the walk.

BRETHERDALE BRIDGE   T. Baynes.

34

Bretherdale and Borrowdale   **15.4km (9.5miles)**

This walk can be combined with Walk No 12 to provide an 18mile figure of eight. The walk visits the less remote side of the Bretherdale valley and combines some rough upland tracks with about two miles of little used country roads. After visiting the hamlet of Roundthwaite, close to the M6 motorway, the return route crosses the bracken clad slopes of Roundthwaite common, where navigation is not easy, before descending steeply into Borrowdale and returning along the valley floor. Leave a car, or descend from the Shap bus (term time only) at the layby on the A6 just south of Huck's Bridge (NY552038).

Start

Walk down the road and just beyond Huck's Bridge go through the gate on the right and follow the river bank past two cross walls to where, opposite some very inadequate stepping stones, a bridleway goes half left, steeply up the fell side. This is the Breasthigh road, and is not hard to follow as it crosses the ridge and descends into the Bretherdale valley. On the descent the only tricky part is near the beginning of Bretherdale Beck, where there appear to be three paths to choose from. Take the middle route that crosses a tributary by a stone bridge and then follows close by the right-hand side of the main beck until it reaches the metalled drive to Bretherdale Head Farm. (This is the point where the 200m link to Walk No 12 can be made along the farm drive.)

Borrowdale   Ian Brodie

1   Turn right and continue alongside the beck on the metalled drive to reach a fenced county road at Midwath Stead Farm. Turn right along the road for about 1.3km. Beyond Bretherdale Hall, the next farm on the left, a drive goes up on the right. Follow the drive to Bretherdale Foot, a converted farmhouse, bear left along the drive and go through two gates beyond the buildings. Go half left across the field to another field gate, and then keep round the right-hand side of the next field to find a stile and a small footbridge over a beck. Cross the bridge and go straight up the field to the farm ahead, Dyke Farm, reaching the farmyard through the field gate just left of the house. (Jennie Hill, is glad to offer refreshments here, if you give her warning the day before. Tel: 015396 24503. A small charge will be made but anything above the cost will go to an appropriate charity) Bear left in the farmyard and follow the drive to the road (Pikestone Lane). The farm drive is not a right of way but the owner has given permission to use it.

2   Turn right along the road for about 1km, and just as a beck emerges to run alongside on the right of the road, look for a signpost to Roundthwaite and a small gate. This leads to a footbridge. Cross the bridge and bear half right to the diagonally opposite corner of the field. Pass through a gate between two walls and then follow the wall on the right to reach a drive. A little way along the drive, a stile on the right leads down a small field to a footbridge over Roundthwaite Beck. After crossing this turn right, then left, then right again, all in quick succession, to gain the bridleway that starts alongside a wall on the right and leads up the fell to a gate in a fence.

3   Follow the wall on your right until it turns away sharply down the hill, then, ignoring a track that goes half left up the fell, continue along the contours, aiming for the right-hand side of a small valley ahead with bracken covered banks. Go above the bracken slope and over the low grassy hill until reaching a wet patch of ground. Cross this and after about another 150 metres follow the track as it swings left near some rock outcrops where a small cairn marks a junction with another track. Ignore this and keep bearing left to go up the right side of a small valley and cross the ridge at the col on the right of Belt Howe, the nearest high point on the ridge.

4   On reaching the top of the col the path becomes more obvious and descends quite steeply to reach Low Borrowdale Farm, the only occupied farm in the Borrowdale valley. Do not go into the farmyard but continue on the cart track below the trees keeping right at a junction. The path soon becomes grassy and passes the ruined High Borrowdale Farm via gates. Eventually you reach a bridge over the beck, and a hard track leads for a further mile or so back to the A6 and the start of the walk.

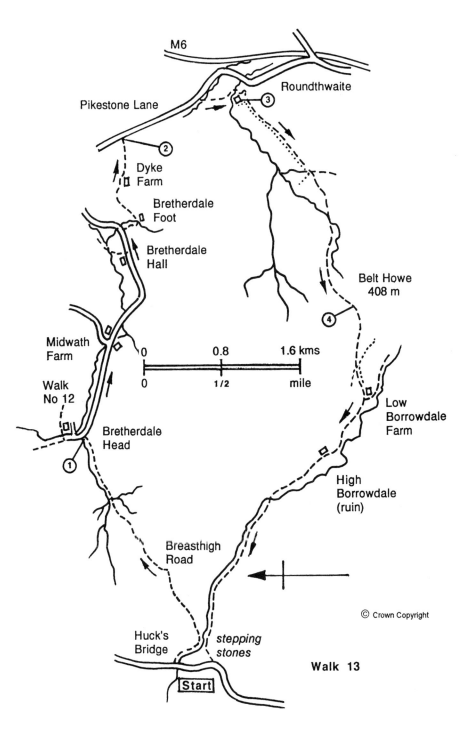

M6

Roundthwaite

Pikestone Lane

② Dyke Farm

③

Bretherdale Foot

Bretherdale Hall

Belt Howe 408 m

④

Midwath Farm

0   0.8   1.6 kms

Walk No 12

0   1/2   mile

Bretherdale Head

①

Low Borrowdale Farm

High Borrowdale (ruin)

Breasthigh Road

© Crown Copyright

Huck's Bridge

stepping stones

Walk 13

Start

Old Hutton and Millholme   14.5km (9miles)

This walk is through gently undulating pastoral scenery, with many wild flowers in the lanes in spring and summer. There are many silage fields, so the walk is not recommended when the grass is long in early summer to avoid trampling the crop, an important part of the local economy. The start of the walk is at SD536864 on the A65, 5 miles south of Kendal. There are two bus stop lay-bys at Summerlands, about ½ mile south of the Halfpenny turning and another lay-by just south of the bus stops, where a car may be parked.

Start
From the bus stop follow the bridleway signposted Birkrigg until it emerges into a field. Continue between the two mounds ahead, bearing slightly right and downhill to go through a small gate in the corner of the field, leading out onto a lane. Turn left along the road for a few metres and go up the drive of Low Park on the right, signposted Footpath to Holmescales. Go straight through the garden to a wooden stile over a low fence leading to a field. Continue by the boundary on the left until reaching Urchinrigg, and go through a field gate on to the drive of the house. Keep round the right-hand side and along the back of the buildings, over the lawn, left of a row of cyprus trees and right of the greenhouse, to leave by another field gate to the north of the property. (This route is a diversion from the right of way, requested by the occupants but not yet official). Continue along the field with the hedge/wall on the right through two field gates, keeping in the same northerly direction to reach Peasey Beck on your right. Follow the beck upstream for about 500m, crossing a number of stiles, until reaching a footbridge. Cross the bridge and go by the side of the wall along two fields to reach a road.

1   Turn left and follow the road for about 700m, then turn left into Popplemire Lane just beyond Holmescales Farm and Riding Centre. Continue for another 600m to the next farm, Ellenwray. Go through the gate on the right opposite the converted barn and head diagonally left across the field to a wooden stile over a fence in the dip. Now aim for the left of the buildings seen ahead, and emerge onto a road at Beckside by a field gate.

2   Turn right, and bearing right at the junction, follow the road for about 250m to a wall gap stile in the corner of the field on the left. Aim diagonally left across this rough pasture to another stile above the cascades of Peasey Beck. After crossing another field and a gap stile keep along the contours to reach the B6254 road at Old Hutton by following the waymarked route round the right of the buildings and through another garden. (A short cut, reducing the walk by about 5 km, may be taken here by continuing along this road to the left for just under 1 km, as far as Middleshaw Bridge. Omit the next 3 paragraphs if doing this and go to para 6).

3   Turn left along the road for 250m to a footpath sign on the right, to Eskrigg End, one field beyond the last house. Go through the field gate and after 50m another one on the right, then follow the field boundary uphill to a wooden stile.

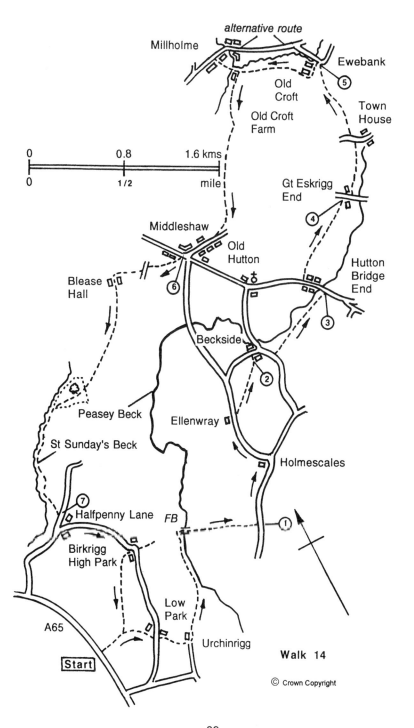

alternative route

Millholme

Ewebank

⑤

Old
Croft

Town
House

Old Croft
Farm

0   0.8   1.6 kms
0   1/2   mile

Gt Eskrigg
End

④

Middleshaw

Old
Hutton

Hutton
Bridge
End

Blease
Hall

⑥

③

Beckside

②

Peasey Beck

Ellenwray

St Sunday's Beck

Holmescales

⑦ Halfpenny Lane

FB

①

Birkrigg
High Park

Low
Park

A65

Urchinrigg

Walk 14

Start

© Crown Copyright

39

below a clump of trees. Keep by the trees on the left to another gate, then contour along the next field with a minor power line on your left, to a waymarked stile, continuing by the boundary on the left across two more fields to reach Eskrigg End via a farmyard.

4   Turn right on the road to where, just past Great Eskrigg End House, a sign on the garage wall indicates the right of way. Go through an iron gate in the corner of the garage court and follow a gravel path through the garden to a small gate beside the shed, leading to a field. Bear right to a field gate, then aim uphill to another field-gate and a ladder stile seen ahead. Continue along the next field, keeping by the hedge on the right, to reach the drive to Town House Farm through a gate near a cattle grid. Cross the cattle grid and very soon, where the drive bears left, go diagonally off right, across the field to a gate in the far corner. Through the gate bear left between two pylons to another gate. Continue to a wooden stile then follow the same line to reach a gate at the bottom of the field, right of the converted farm buildings at Ewebank, and emerge onto another road.

5   Bear left, following the Ewebank sign, and after a left-hand bend, follow a bridleway sign on the right to Old Croft. Keep left of the converted barn and along the back of it to reach a fenced path going into a narrow hedged lane. This is very wet underfoot and apt to be overgrown in summer, but it can be avoided by following the road through Millholme hamlet - see map. The hedged green lane continues for about 200m then opens into a field. Keep by the hedge on the right down to Old Croft Farm, passing through a field gate. Just before the barn turn left, then right, behind the barn, into a yard. Cross the yard diagonally to a gate and stile into a field, and continue with the hedge on your right. Just before the end of the second field bear slightly left to a high step stile. After crossing this go up the cart track by the hedge to a gate at the next bend. (A beef bull may be grazing with cows in this last field during the summer months). Continue along the hedge on the right to the next field, and cross a stile and gate to follow a thin hedge on the left. Now keep straight ahead as far as a ladder stile under the first pylon line. Keep at the same level in the next field, cross a stile and continue to reach a gate, then follow the old rutted track across the field towards the houses seen ahead. A rough track below the bungalow leads to a finger post and a narrow lane. Turn right along the lane past Middleshaw Hall to reach the B6254 again at the northern end of Old Hutton village.

6   If you have decided to cut out the last three paragraphs rejoin the walk here. At Middleshaw Bridge take the 'Footpath' signed path between the houses, and on reaching a field keep by the hedge on your right to a gate. Continue over the hill by the wall to reach a narrow green lane. Turn left for a few metres to a stile on the right into the corner of the field opposite. You are now entering farmland that is protected by low voltage electric wires close to walls and hedges. If you accidentally touch these wires you can get quite a nasty shock, as the writer of this walk did! Keep the wall/hedge on your left over the next hill, a drumlin, to descend to Blease Hall Farm via a path at the edge of the garden of a modern bungalow. Blease Hall, built about 1600AD is one of the finest old farmhouses in this area. Keep straight ahead across the drive and through the trees to find a small gap stile

in the corner behind a large tree, left of a hut. Turn left and go through the long farmyard to leave it by a rough lane at the far end. Follow this track, bearing right along the wall on reaching a field. Pass through a gate and in the next field keep the field boundary on your left and pass through another gate. Beyond the gate bear half right across the field to find a small plank bridge and ladder stile over a watercourse at the right end of the facing wall. Keep straight ahead to a kissing gate into the wood opposite, where many young trees have been planted, and follow the broad track to an iron stile at the far side. After crossing the stile continue along beside St Sunday's Beck on the right for about 1km, crossing a number of stiles and eventually emerging via a field gate onto a narrow lane at Halfpenny.

7   Turn right along the lane to the next junction, then turn left and follow another lane for 800m to reach Birkrigg High Park. Follow the road round past the main farmhouse and turn right at the signpost to Storth End, going between a modern shed and the horse-schooling yard. At the end of the shed turn left, and then right, to reach an old bridleway. Follow this to the left, through the wood. On reaching a field keep by the wall on your left along two fields, bearing slightly right at the end of the second one to re-enter the bridleway where the walk started via a high step stile. Turn right for the starting point.

BLEASE HALL

M. Adams.

WALK NO. 15

Howgill Fells and Upper Lune Valley   16km (10miles)

The Howgill Fells, between the eastern Lakeland fells and the Yorkshire Dales and Pennines form a compact mass of rounded hills separated by very steep-sided valleys. They give magnificent views of the neighbouring hills and the coastal area around Morecambe Bay. The dry and grassy hills make easy walking, but the absence of distinguishing landmarks and the general similarity of the ridges and valleys makes for demanding navigation in mist. This walk over the southwest facing ridges rises to a maximum height of 2200ft and is best attempted on a clear day. The walk starts on the main Kendal to Sedbergh road (A684) at SD634922, about 500m east of Lincoln's Inn Bridge, the single lane bridge crossing the Lune. Park in a lay-by beside the old St Gregory's Church on the right-hand side of the road. The start is on the route of the Kendal to Sedbergh bus service.

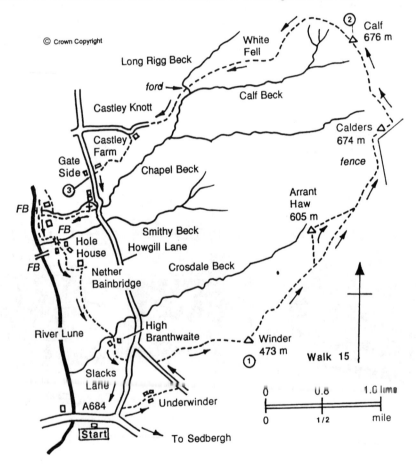

42

Start

Walk along the road towards Sedbergh and take the first turning on the left, Slacks Lane. After a few metres go up the drive on the right to the buildings of Underwinder. Go to the right, rearside of the converted barn (Greenmantle) then continue through a gate and up, to cross a stile into a field. Keep by the left-hand boundary of two fields to reach Howgill Lane. Turn left along the road for 450m to a signpost on the right to Brant Fell; this enclosed track leads to the open fell via a gate. Go right then left up the fell aiming for the high ground ahead, and before long you should join a good track that leads direct to the summit of Winder with its trig point at 473m (1551ft).

1   From the trig point on a clear day the route ahead is plainly visible, climbing over the shoulder of Arrant Haw. Follow the well-trodden path, bearing right at a fork. (A detour is possible to the top of Arrant Haw, rejoining the main route further on). After passing beyond Arrant Haw climb steeply beside a wire fence to the top of Calders.   At the summit, which is marked by a low cairn, leave the wire fence on the right and turn left to join another clear track that can be seen ahead, rising to the trig point at the top of the Calf, the highest point in the Howgills at 676m (2220ft).

2   From the Calf keep going straight ahead in a north-westerly direction, ignoring the track going off right, to pick up a clear track that follows the ridge of White Fell round to the left in a gentle curve. Soon the track descends quite steeply and about 1.5miles from the Calf summit you reach a ford (hopefully not too deep) at the confluence of Calf beck and Long Rigg beck. Continue along the track over the flank of Castley Knott to reach a walled lane by a gate just above some sheep pens, that leads to Castley Farm. At the farm follow the sign to Gate Side, left, down the farm drive. Bear right past the farmhouse, and right again to enter a field through a gate. Continue along the track across the field to another gate and go up to a gap in the next wall and a sign pointing right to a ladder stile. From the stile go straight across the field to join a track going left towards Gate Side Farm. After a gate, keep round the left of the buildings to a stile out onto Howgill Lane (an old Roman road).

3   You could follow the Roman road left for just over two miles, all the way back to Slacks Lane, near the start. But a more interesting and slightly longer route follows the river bank and field paths. Go left along the lane for 400m, but immediately after crossing the bridge over Chapel Beck go through a gate on the right and down the road past Howgill Church and some converted mill buildings. Keep right at the fork and continue by the beck, leaving the road immediately before it crosses a bridge to Beckside Farm, to go left onto a grassy track beside the beck. Follow the beck, passing through a gate, to where it joins the River Lune near a footbridge. Don't cross the bridge but turn left and follow the riverbank round to where a fence blocks your way. Go left and follow the fence and cross a stile in the next corner, then follow the beckside path up to a footbridge. Cross the bridge and go straight ahead between the buildings of Hole House Farm and through the gated farmyards. At the top of the yards, after the third gate, is a signpost. Go right to climb the knoll and on to reach a gate in the wall where it meets a fence. Through this follow the

left-hand wall to a signpost at the next farm, Nether Bainbridge. Go right in front of the buildings, but soon turn left over a wall stile and turn right into a lane. Follow this, keeping in the same direction past a small barn. Continue uphill gradually nearing the overhead wires, to cross a stile in a wall corner near an electricity pole. Continue by the left-hand field boundary to another wall stile, then cross the field to a gate just left of a hen house. Go through the gate and follow the boundary to the left of the buildings, keeping by the right-hand wall after the enclosed track reaches a field. Soon you reach another footbridge, leading over Crosdale Beck to High Branthwaite Farm. Go through the farmyard, leaving by the gate ahead, then, after a few paces, bear left at a junction and enter a field by a gate. Cross the field by the wall on the left to a wooden stile in the corner. Now aim for a signpost half left to go over a ruined wall and straight up the hill to reach Slacks Lane again by a stone wall stile. Turn right for half a mile down the road to the starting point.

WALK NO. 16

Middleton Fell and the Lune Valley   21km or 12km   (13 or 7.5 miles)

This varied walk involves a fairly strenuous climb up to a maximum height of 609m (1999ft) from where you are rewarded by splendid all round views. There is a good long ridge walk on the longer version of the walk and a pleasant return through the pastures of the Lune valley. Do choose a clear day, not only to get the best views but also because the narrow path along the ridge tends to be seasonal and you may well lose it in mist before the security of the guiding wall is reached. There are few landmarks. Remember it will be considerably colder on top. There is plenty of room to park near the very beautiful late 19th Century church at Barbon, north of Kirkby Lonsdale, off the A683.

BARBON CHURCH   M. Adams

Start

Leave the village by the road to the Manor, on the left just beyond the church. Cross the cattle grid and bridge and after approx. 120m leave the road at the right-hand bend, to head straight across the park towards the right-hand side of the wood ahead. Keep alongside the wood to reach a gate into a field before Eskholme Farm then head half right up the field to another gate near some mature trees. Go up the fell, bearing slightly right towards a wall, to cross some crags and reach the cairn at Eskholme Pike (307m). From here a narrow path (not always clear) starts and continues for 2km over rising ground, past another small cairn, to reach a large cairn on Castle Knott. The path now dips down over wetter ground before rising again onto the Calf and reaching a wall corner (the boundary of the Yorkshire Dales National Park). Continue along by the wall to reach the trig point on Calf Top at 609m (1999ft). From here on a clear day the view takes in Ingleborough (SE), the Forest of Bowland, Morecambe Bay and the Lancashire Coast to the south. The Furness peninsular lies to the SW and a panorama of the Lakeland fells is seen to the west, going round to the Howgills in the north with Sedbergh town nestling below them. Dentdale lies to the NW.

The choice between longer and shorter routes starts from this summit. If you are doing the 13mile circuit omit the next paragraph.

THE SHORTER ROUTE

Turn sharply left away from the wall and trig point and aim for the highest ground to the west, across rough moorland until very shortly, you join a grassy vehicular track. Follow this as it snakes over the fell and gradually descends on a winding route for about 3.5km to reach Mill House farm. This is not a right of way but should present no problems as there are no walls or fences until you reach the farm at Mill House. Go through several gated sheep pens and find a stone wall stile on the left between the first two outbuildings, leading to a bridge over the beck. Omit the next three paragraphs and go to paragraph 4.

THE LONGER ROUTE

1   From Calf Top continue alongside the wall on the right on a fairly distinct track for about 3.5km (2.25miles), after which the track leaves the wall. After a further 2.5km and crossing several fords over small streams you reach Fellside Farm. From here the farm drive descends to the main road through a delightful nature reserve with many flowers in spring and summer.

2   The Head Inn, serving bar food, is now about 400m to the left should you require refreshments, but otherwise turn right along the A683 for 150m then go through a gate on the left and through a wood on a track leading down to the River Lune. Just before reaching a gate into a field bear left and continue along the bottom of the wood to another gate into a field. Go along the bottom of the field then bear right towards a barn. Go through the gate left of the barn and keep by the hedge on the left until approaching Waterside Farm, then go down a small path to the riverbank, the site of a former ford, and climb up behind the farmhouse to a gate into the yard. Continuing in the same southerly direction go through a gate into a fenced track, at the end of which you take the right-hand of two gates, leading into

a field. Continue by the fence/hedge on the left passing through two gates, until reaching a large open field. Cross this to the far left-hand corner, where a gate gives access to the A683 again, opposite the drive to Middleton Hall Farm, a fine example of a 15th Century fortified farmhouse.

3   Take the minor road, signposted High Green, beside the entrance to the farm. From here it is possible to follow this very quiet road for about 5km all the way back to the starting point at Barbon. This may be desirable at times when the fields are full of long grass. However, for a more adventurous route, slightly longer and involving a little climbing, follow the minor road for approx. 800m. Then, 220m after crossing the beck, ignore a minor road on the right, and go through a stile on the left at the right-hand bend in the road, leading straight ahead into a field. Cross the field, aiming towards Ullathorns seen ahead. Go through the right-hand gate in the corner of the field and another leading into the yard in front of the farmhouse. Turn right between the buildings and go through the right-hand gateway leading to the farm drive. Now go through another gate straight ahead leading into a field and follow the wall on the left until it turns away at a corner. Bear half left towards the next farm, Tossbeck, entering the yard by a field gate. Turn left in front of the gable end of the farmhouse and go up the yard to an archway under the old railway line. On emerging from the underpass cross a concrete slab bridge, and then keep right, parallel to the old railway to find a stile in the next wall. Cross the field to another wall stile, then go down to a gate and stile in the left-hand corner of the next field, bearing sharp left to the next stile. Now go diagonally right to a stile in the internal corner of the next wall, and having crossed this continue on the same line towards the trees over the brow of the hill, to reach a stile adjacent to a gate. Still on the same line, aim for a stile at the junction of wall and fence ahead, leading to the Mill House Farm road. Go up the road to the farm and through a gate on the left of the main buildings. Now go up the yard to find a stile between the last two out buildings on the right, leading to a bridge over the beck.

4   The longer and shorter walks now return by the same route. After crossing the beck at Mill House Farm go through the gate 25m right of the barn ahead, then make a beeline for the roofs that can be seen over the brow of the hill in front. On reaching this farm, Low Fellside, cross a wall stile into a horse paddock and keep left of the buildings to a field gate, then continue past an old barn on the right, down to another gate. Now keep along the bottom of two fields and round the left and far sides of the third to reach another barn. Go through the gate in the corner of the field, and follow the stony track to where it goes alongside the old railway embankment to reach Sowermire Farm through an archway. Bear left in front of the farmhouse (watch out for a tethered dog jumping out on turning the corner). Follow the drive down for about 20m to cross a stile on the left at the corner of a wood. Cross the small footbridge over the beck, then aim between the two large trees seen ahead to an old gateway. After this veer left towards the next and last farm, Borwens. About five dogs, all mercifully chained up but barking furiously, defend this! Pass in front of the farmhouse and bear right through a gate at the end of the yard to cross a small field diagonally to a stile onto a minor road. Follow this road left for about 1km back to Barbon.

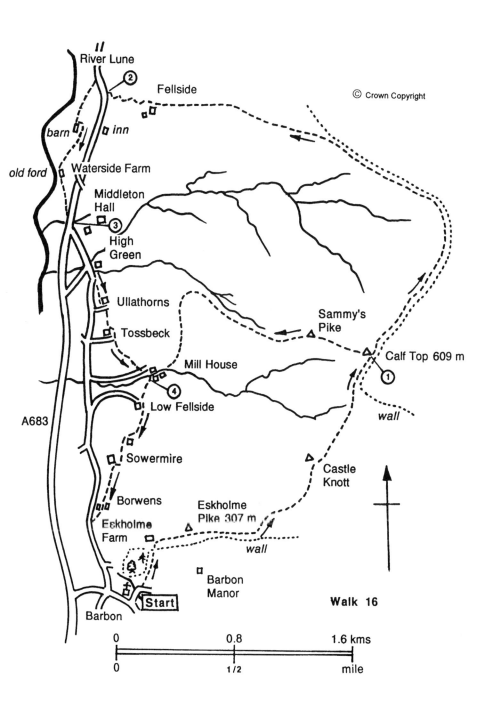

River Lune

② Fellside

© Crown Copyright

barn inn

old ford Waterside Farm

Middleton Hall
③

High Green

Ullathorns

Tossbeck

Mill House

④

Low Fellside

A683

Sowermire

Borwens

Eskholme Farm

Sammy's Pike

Calf Top 609 m
①

wall

Castle Knott

Eskholme Pike 307 m

wall

Barbon Manor

Walk 16

Start

Barbon

0	0.8	1.6 kms
0	1/2	mile

WALK NO. 17

Longsleddale   20km or 7km (12 or 4.75 miles)

The valley of Longsleddale, north of Kendal, is an area of great beauty in the Lake District National Park, and still relatively unfrequented by walkers. The lush green pastures in the bottom of the valley are 'in-bye' grazing for numerous sheep and cattle - please take special care to control dogs and leave gates as found. The longer walk also includes stretches of wild and desolate moorland to the west of the valley. This is not country to venture into when there is mist, as there are many boggy areas and the track is not clear in places. However, it can be a rewarding walk at all times of the year, not least when the heather is in bloom in August. The walk begins near Watchgate on the A6 road about 4 miles north of Kendal, at SD527989. There are occasional buses to Shap passing this way; otherwise park the car at the lay-by next to the telephone kiosk, 300m north of the road sign to Longsleddale. Some of the walk is on bridleways marked by blue arrows on a yellow background, though in some cases the blue may have faded away.

Start
Walk northwards on this normally quiet main road for 0.8km (0.5mile) ignoring the bridleway on the left, to reach the first metalled lane on the left, by an electricity substation building. After about 200m along this road turn left onto a side road that goes to Mosergh Farm. Just before the farm turn right onto a walled bridleway and continue for 700m, passing a track on the right, before reaching another bridleway sign to the left. The cairned peak ahead is Whiteside Pike. Through the gate on the left follow the track until it opens into a field, where marker posts show the way ahead. Drop down to the wall at the bottom of the field, bearing left to a small gate near a plantation. Through this gate a notice indicates that access to the area adjoining the bridleway is available under the Countryside Stewardship scheme for a limited period. If you are doing the shorter walk you may like to climb to the top of Murthwaite Knott, seen ahead, to enjoy the view up the valley. Otherwise continue down the bridleway to arrive at the valley road via Murthwaite Farm.

1   Turn right along the road for 800m, passing Low House Farm on the right. Take note of this, as it will be a useful marker to aim for on the return route, as you cross the moorland on the other side of the valley. You reach another bridleway sign on the left about 400m after passing the entrance to Low House Farm. Cross the bridge over the River Sprint on the farm track to Docker Nook. Shortly after the bridge the short and long walks divide; if doing the longer walk omit the next paragraph.

THE SHORTER WALK
A few metres along the farm track go through the first gate on the left and walk across the field, aiming for the farm seen ahead, to an iron gate that leads onto a good track that goes past the farm, Bridge End. To continue go to paragraph 8.

THE LONGER WALK
2   Continue along the farm track to a gate into the field in front of the farm.

Through the gate turn sharp right and go through the right-hand of two gates seen ahead, and follow the green track beside the wire fence. The route is easy to follow as it passes through gates with the wall/fence on one side, then on the other.

LONGSLEDDALE   T. Baynes.

3   At Kilnstones, the next farm to be reached, the gate is at the left-hand end of the barn, after which the wall is on your left.   When Beech Hill Farm (now converted) comes into view take the left-hand of two gates and continue with the wall on your right. Go past Beech Hill, with Longsleddale Church visible beyond the river, go through the small gate ahead, and then bear right, steeply down towards the beck (NOT the gate just ahead) to continue with the wall on your left to another gate. Cross the middle of the next four fields to reach Wad's Howe.

4   At Wad's Howe follow the signs to the right onto the farm drive, and then go through the gate on the left just below the farmhouse, near a telegraph pole. Continue with the wall/fence on your left to Hollin Root, another recently converted farmhouse. Just before Hollin Root turn up left to a field gate to leave the valley and ascend to the moorland. The broad stony track winds up the hillside for about 500m, passing through a gate near a ruined building. Ignore the gate onto the moor immediately on your left and carry on with the wall on your left until reaching a kissing gate onto the moor higher up. Now keep near the wall on the left at first, between stone grouse butts, gradually leaving the wall to cross some boggy ground. A marker post on the track ahead points left, and the track becomes easier to follow from here. Glimpses of the lonely tarn of Skeggleswater can soon be seen

over on the right. The track continues across the moor for about 1.6km (1mile), first passing through a gateway in a wall, then crossing Skeggleswater Dyke that flows from the tarn to become a tributary of the River Kent. At the second wall you leave the heather moorland through a gate giving access to rough pasture and bracken slopes; green fields lie ahead.

5   At a small cairn near a ruined barn you join the track coming down from Green Quarter Fell above Kentmere. As the track snakes away southwards the upper reaches of Morecambe Bay can be seen in the distance, while the Kentmere valley lies over on the right. Keep on descending gradually as the track goes between walls and eventually becomes a tarmac road. Follow this past Park House riding centre and on downhill for another 750m; at an S bend the road goes over a beck and immediately beyond it a footpath sign points over a stile on the left.

6   Go uphill beside the beck, crossing two stiles, to reach the drive below Ghyll Bank, the large white house. Turn right and cross the cattle grid, continuing along the road and over another cattle grid. Now turn sharp left, up the drive to Brunt Knott Farm. Go up between the buildings and follow the track uphill, crossing a ladder stile and taking the right fork, which eventually leads alongside the wall. Keep by this wall on the right for about 200m, following the old green sunken track and ignoring the gate into the field and various modern tractor tracks branching left. The green track leaves the wall at a boggy area and soon a stile can be seen on the right, over a wire fence. Two faint tracks start on the far side of the stile. Take the left one that goes round the marsh ahead, and carry on until you're opposite a ladder stile in the wall on the right. Here the path turns right to reach the stile.

7   After crossing the ladder stile bear half left to follow a fairly distinct track going along a low ridge between two watercourses. Dockernook Gill soon becomes dominant on the left, whilst the track bears right across watercourses flowing down to the Gill. Continue on the track for about another 500m, and where the track forks take the left-hand fork, aiming towards Low House Farm (passed on the outward route) seen ahead across the Longsleddale valley.   Continue down this path between the bracken, eventually reaching a wall and following it right, on a sunken track, to descend to Bridge End Farm down a steep field. Turn right at the gate onto the farm drive.

8   Continue on the track past Tenter Howe (ruined) and Tenter House Farms. One field past Nether House, and before the bridge, turn off right through a signed gate and go alongside the beck to reach a field. Go by the wall on your right and take the right-hand of two gates into the next field. Now keep by the wall on the left, uphill to another gate, and descend the following field to cross the end of the drive to Cocks Close on your left. Continue with the wall/fence on your left to reach an enclosed green lane leading to the hamlet of Garnett Bridge. Cross the bridge and turn right up the hill for 360m (ignoring a bridleway on the left) to a footpath sign to Garnett Plains. Go up by the wall on the right to reach the starting point over a ladder stile.

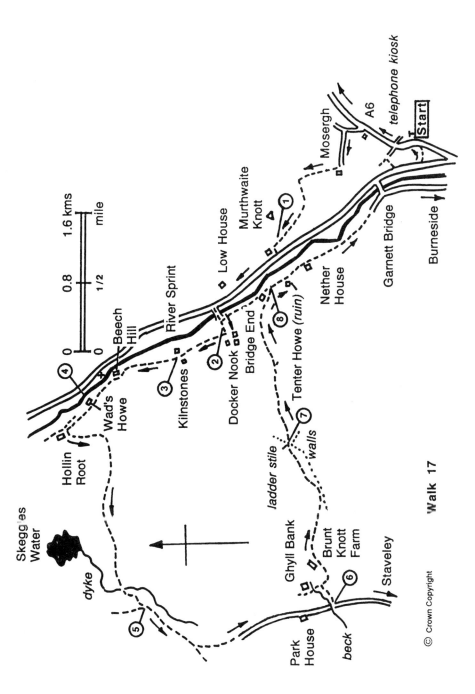

Walk 17

© Crown Copyright

WALK NO. 18

Kendal to Kirkby Lonsdale   24km (15 miles)

Starting beside the River Kent and finishing by the River Lune, this walk links the two market towns of Kendal and Kirkby Lonsdale by a mixture of riverside paths, old canal towpaths, field paths, and ancient bridleways and quiet country roads where good progress can be made. You can get refreshments at either the Crooklands Hotel or at the Plough Inn at Lupton, which is just off the route. Both are near the halfway point and the walk could be split into two here. Buses are infrequent, so it is necessary to make inquiries about the return journey before setting out. Allow seven hours walking time.

Start

From Nether Bridge in Kendal, follow the west bank of the River Kent along Milnthorpe Rd. bearing left after 100m into South Road, to reach Romney Bridge by a riverside path that starts before the houses on the left. Cross the bridge and turn right into Natland Road. Continue for about 600m, and then follow a footpath sign to Hawes Bridge on the right, between the last house and a factory building. On approaching the river turn left through the car park behind the buildings and go up the steps behind the boiler house and large tank, to emerge onto a drive. Turn right towards the former Watercrook Farm, site of a Roman fort, and cross the stile in the wire fence on the left. Now bear half right to go round the right-hand end of the higher ground ahead, close to the riverbank where you may see a dipper, then aim for a squeeze stile seen ahead. From here follow the pleasant river bank path for 1.25km to Natland Lane.

1   On reaching the lane turn right for a few metres and cross the stile on the left just before Hawes Bridge where the river passes through a small gorge. Continue on the left bank of the river for about 1km until, just past a farm over on the left, you emerge onto an enclosed bridleway. Follow the bridleway left, back towards the farm. On reaching a field climb half right, up to a bridge over the former Lancaster canal. Pass through a stone stile before the bridge and follow the former towpath to the right. After going through the wood keep to the same line across the reinstated fields passing under another fine old canal bridge and eventually arriving at the village of Sedgwick. Just before the old canal crosses the road go down a flight of stone steps on the right and turn left along the road under the bridge.

2   Follow the road through Sedgwick, turning right at the signpost to Crosscrake and Endmoor, and continue on for about 700m to a crossroads immediately before Crosscrake Church. Turn right (marked to Stainton Cross) and go through a large field gate a few metres along on the left. Now head diagonally across the field to a gate and stile in the far right-hand corner. Keep alongside the hedge on the left in the next field, but where the ground begins to drop bear half right to a ladder stile in a short piece of wall. Now follow the wall/hedge on the left up to the top of Skettlegill Hill, a drumlin. Continue on the same line to drop down to the gate at Skettlegill Farm. Bear right through the farmyard to the road.

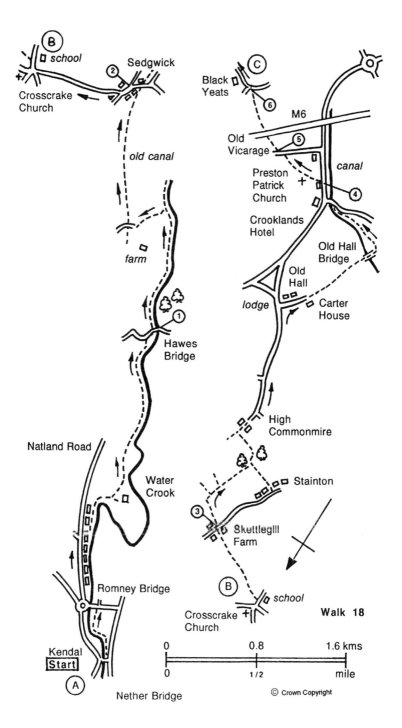

B

□ school

Sedgwick

②

Crosscrake
Church

old canal

farm

①

Hawes
Bridge

Natland Road

Water
Crook

Romney Bridge

Kendal
Start

A

Nether Bridge

Black
Yeats

C

⑥

M6

Old
Vicarage

⑤

Preston
Patrick
Church

✝

canal

④

Crooklands
Hotel

Old Hall
Bridge

Old
Hall

lodge

Carter
House

High
Commonmire

Stainton

③

Skettlegill
Farm

B

□ school

Crosscrake
Church

Walk 18

0	0.8	1.6 kms
0	1/2	mile

© Crown Copyright

53

3   Cross the road to the gate opposite and keep straight ahead up the field to a wooden stile in the hedge. Turn partly left and go down to a difficult stile, not immediately seen, in the far right-hand corner of the second field. Continue up the wall on the right as far as it goes, then continue up the field to the wall at the top. Turn right along the wall to a stile on the left, emerging at a bend in a lane. Go straight ahead along the lane, passing a wood on the right and when a field is met, pass to the left of it to a metal waymarked gate. The route passes down the wood veering to the left to a stone stile. Go straight up the field to a gate and stile opposite. Turn right along the bridleway (ignore a stile on the left) to reach a narrow road at High Commonmire Farm. Follow this road for about 1km, ignoring a turning on the right, a road on the left and another footpath on the left. On reaching 'North Lodge', turn down the lane on the right, SP Crooklands, and follow it past Carter House Farm on the right. About 250m beyond the farm, go through the left-hand of three field gates with a barn on the left and a water tank on the right. Keep alongside the hedge on the right to reach Old Hall Bridge, where you rejoin the old Lancaster canal, which here still holds water. Cross the bridge, go down to the towpath and follow it to Crooklands, leaving it by a small opening onto the road beside what used to be a barge horse stable, now occupied by the Canal Preservation Trust. Turn left along the road and go over the bridge near the Crooklands Hotel.

4   Turn right along the A65, and just beyond the filling station on the left you will find steps leading up to a path to Preston Patrick Church. The church was rebuilt in 1852 and with its illuminated cross at night is a landmark for travellers along the busy M6, A591 and A65 roads. On reaching the church keep along the bottom of the churchyard to a second kissing gate, then turn left along the wall to emerge onto a road beside the former vicarage.

5   Cross slightly left to a footbridge over a small beck, then head across the field to go through a narrow cattle creep, which can be seen going under the motorway. Beyond this is a stile across the field. Continue on by the wall/hedge on the right to reach a gate onto a minor road.

6   Bear left up the minor road, passing Black Yeats Farm to reach a T-junction after 450m, then turn right for 150m to a bridleway on the left. Follow the bridleway for 450m to where it turns fairly sharply to the left, with a stile in the wall facing you. Do not cross the stile but go though the gate on the right and immediately turn left, round the gorse bushes, to ford a small beck. Go up the field then aim right for the far bottom corner of Highlander Wood. Pass round the southern edge of the wood to find a stile, and continue along the boundary on the right across the next three fields. Enter the fourth field by a gate and pass around the right-hand edge to emerge onto a farm lane through another gate.

7   Turn right down the lane for a few metres (or all the way to the bottom and the A65 If you want to visit the Plough Inn - see map), then go through the yard of Crabtree Farm, leaving by a gate into a wide hedged lane. At the end go through the right-hand gate into a field turning left to continue along a level grassy bank to another gate. Keep by the hedge on the left across the next field to find a stile in the fence beside a large ash tree with a small stone footbridge beyond, leading

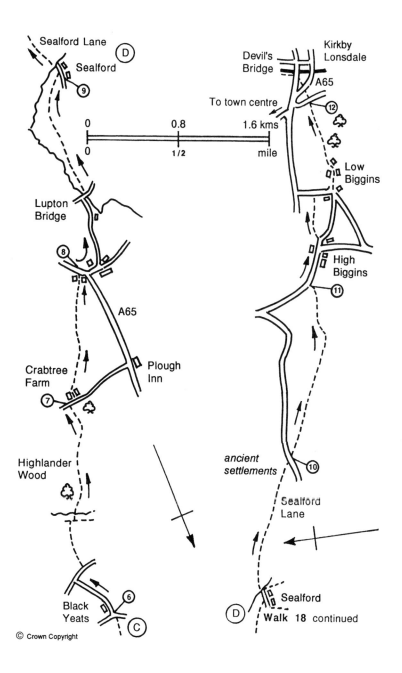

Sealford Lane

Sealford

(D)

(9)

Kirkby
Lonsdale

Devil's
Bridge

A65

To town centre

(12)

0   0.8   1.6 kms

0   1/2   mile

Low
Biggins

Lupton
Bridge

(8)

High
Biggins

A65

(11)

Crabtree
Farm

Plough
Inn

(7)

Highlander
Wood

*ancient
settlements*

(10)

Sealford
Lane

Black
Yeats

(6)

(C)

(D) Sealford

Walk 18 continued

© Crown Copyright

into the corner of the third field. Now go diagonally down this field to a gate in the opposite lower corner, crossing the next small field to a stone gap stile. From here the path leads straight ahead between the buildings to the main road (A65).

8   Turn right for a few metres and go down the minor road opposite, taking the first turn off it on the left after 150m. Follow this road for about 600m to Lupton Bridge. Cross the bridge and go through the stile on the left immediately beyond it, signposted Sealford. Keep along the bottom of this field at first, near the beck, and then aim for the freestanding old gatepost in the middle of the field, that marks the line of the path. Beyond this gatepost aim for a waymarked wooden stile halfway up the next hedge. Continue climbing to the far corner of the next field to another way-marked stile then carry on by the fence on the left, bearing right across the higher ground after 250m to reach a stile just to the right of the buildings at Sealford Farm.

9   Turn left along Sealford Lane and keep straight ahead into the narrow bridleway. In summer this can get very overgrown with nettles, etc, and it may be necessary to sidetrack into the fields on the left, but remember that strictly speaking this is trespassing and your passage is dependent on the good will of the farmer. After about 500m the bridleway loses its hedges and continues across open pasture. Follow the same direction past marker posts and through a gate by an electricity pole. Cross the next field to a gate into a metalled lane, near the site of an ancient settlement.

10   Cross the road to the stile opposite and go half-left across the field to reach a wall. Keep the wall on the left to a gate and continue by the wall across two more fields. When the wall turns away sharply left, keep on beside the uncultivated strip of land to find a stile at the bottom of the third field. Now bear slightly left to reach a stile in the far left corner of the next field. Cross the following field diagonally to a stile close to an electricity pole to emerge onto another metalled lane.

11   Turn right down this lane to High Biggins. Keep straight on at the road junction in High Biggins and take the kissing gate on the left, SP Low Biggins. Follow the well-used path to reach the road at Low Biggins. Turn right for 150m to where the road swings right, and then follow the footpath on the left SP to Devil's Bridge. At the farm turn left in front of the slurry tank into a field. Turn right to go alongside the wood on the right and continue downhill towards Kirkby Lonsdale, emerging onto a road between the second and third pair of houses. Cross over to another path leading to the A65.

12   From here you can turn left and then right into the main street of Kirkby Lonsdale. A more interesting route, taking in some of the main features of the town, continues across the next field to the famous l5th Century Devil's Bridge and then follows the scenic river footpath up stream. After about 1km, steps lead steeply up to the ancient Parish Church and the terrace viewpoint over the Lune, much praised by John Ruskin.